T0305372

PRESIDENTS *and the*
POLITICS OF AGENCY DESIGN

Presidents *and the*

Politics of Agency Design

POLITICAL INSULATION IN THE
UNITED STATES GOVERNMENT
BUREAUCRACY, 1946–1997

David E. Lewis

STANFORD UNIVERSITY PRESS
Stanford, California 2003

Stanford University Press
Stanford, California

© 2003 by the Board of Trustees of the
Leland Stanford Junior University

Printed and bound by CPI Group (UK) Ltd, Croydon, CR0 4YY

Library of Congress Cataloging-in-Publication Data

Lewis, David E.
  Presidents and the politics of agency design : political insulation
in the United States government bureaucracy, 1946–1997 /
David E. Lewis.
      p.   cm.
  Includes bibliographical references and index.
    ISBN 0-8047-4588-9 (hardcover : alk. paper)—
ISBN 0-8047-4590-0 (pbk. : alk. paper)
    1. Administrative agencies—United States.   2. Bureaucracy—
United States.   3. Presidents—United States.   4. United States—
Politics and government—1945–1989.   5. United States—Politics
and government—1989–   I. Title.
JK411 .L49   2003
351.73'09'045—dc21   2002006929

Original Printing 2003

Last figure below indicates year of this printing:
12   11   10   09   08   07   06   05   04   03

Designed by James P. Brommer
Typeset in by Heather Boone in 10.5/14.5 Caslon

For G-ma and G-pa

Contents

Figures and Tables

TABLES

Acknowledgments

This project is the culmination of four years of hard work. Terry Moe originally turned me on to the topic of agency design. Terry's work on the "politics of bureaucratic structure" was this project's starting point. Terry's argument in some ways is simple: the design of administrative agencies is political. Agencies are not designed to be effective, rather they are the result of a political bargain among interested parties. What amazed me throughout my research and what still amazes me is just how prescient, just how right Terry was, not only in the simple truth about the politics of the process, but also in his more complex explanation of how the process works. Terry's imprint is all over this research, the ideas, the writing, and the methods. I'm a better political scientist for Terry's pedagogy, careful criticism, and friendship.

I also benefited from the comments and criticisms of Jon Bendor and John Cogan. I hold Jon Bendor in very high esteem as a teacher and scholar. I consider him a model. I benefited from his comments and criticisms on the theoretical part of this project. I was never fully able to incorporate all his comments and suggestions, and this project is the less for it. John Cogan kindly provided data, his knowledge about the budget process, and methodological insights to the project.

This project benefited from the insightful, penetrating, but friendly criticism of Dick Brody. Dick and I had lunch about once a month during the writing and researching. We sort of had a deal. Dick would show me a good place to eat in Palo Alto, and I would get to ask him about my research. As you can see, this was a pretty lopsided arrangement. To make matters worse, Dick also picked up the check too many times. Dick's knowledge of presidential politics, his ability to go straight to the weaknesses in my argument, and his encouragement were invaluable.

Walt Stone has been a mentor and friend since my time at the University of Colorado. One of his greatest assets is his ability to think clearly and cut away unnecessary material from an argument. He has been a great encouragement to me, making me believe that I could succeed. He has also taught me a lot about what it means to be a professional, coaching me through the publication process, the job process, and grad school. For these things I am grateful. He is a good friend.

Sean Theriault has read just about everything I have written. His boundless optimism and his willingness to share with me the joys and disappointments I've experienced have made this process easier. I am thankful for his friendship, his copyediting, and his keen analytic eye. Some day we will collaborate on something. In the meantime I am more than satisfied just being his friend.

I would also like to thank other friends and colleagues for their encouragement, help, and patience. In particular, Dom Apollon, Kelly Chang, Josh Clinton, Alex George, John Gilmour, Erica Gould, Doug Grob, Will Howell, Simon Jackman, Nolan McCarty, Dan Osborn, Ricardo Ramirez, Ron Rapoport, Michael Strine, Mike Tierney, Shawn Treier, Barry Weingast, and Alan Wiseman all deserve more credit than they are getting here. I would also like to thank my friends at the College of William & Mary, a place where any scholar can have success both as a researcher and as a teacher. I have learned a lot about making a life, a career, and friendships thanks to the Rapoports, McGlennons, Tierneys, Schwartzes, and Bills.

Without resources no project like this succeeds. I am grateful for the financial support of the College of William & Mary, the Stanford University Department of Political Science, the Budde family, the Social Science History Institute, and the Harvey Fellowship Program run by the Mustard Seed Foundation. I appreciate that latter for "marking" me and helping me realize that all this work isn't for me. Thanks also to Amanda Moran and Kate Wahl at Stanford University Press, who adopted the project.

Thanks to my kin for their encouragement: Mom and Johnnye, Dad and Barbara, Ineke and Jos, the West Coast Lewises, Jen, Paul, Pam, and Daniel, and the de Konings. Finally, I am thankful for my wife, Saskia, and my daughter, Julianna, and my new son, little Dave, who are a constant reminder that my life is a success whether I succeed or fail in my chosen profession. I cannot count their numerous allowances, special gifts, and acts of love, but they mean more to me than any book or successful career ever could.

I dedicate this book to my grandparents Lois and Waldo Gossard.

G-ma and G-pa provided loving guidance and instruction to my brother and me throughout our formative years. Their prayers, their example, and their quiet, selfless manner shaped us immensely. I learned about unconditional love from them, and I learned what the scriptures taught by seeing it embodied in their day-to-day lives. I thank God for them.

PRESIDENTS *and the*
POLITICS OF AGENCY DESIGN

Agency Design in American Politics

> In reality, bureaus are among the most important institutions in every part of the world. Not only do they provide employment for a very significant fraction of the world's population; but they also make critical decisions that shape the economic, educational, political, social, moral, and even religious lives of nearly everyone on earth. . . . Yet the role of bureaus in both economic and political theory is hardly commensurate with their true importance.
>
> —Anthony Downs, *Inside Bureaucracy*

Not many people find the study of American bureaucracy a provocative or compelling subject. Discussion of American politics generally revolves around the actions of Congress, the president, and, to a lesser extent, the courts. This oversight is unfortunate. The administrative state is the nexus of policy making in the postwar period. The vague and sometimes conflicting policy mandates of Congress, the president, and courts get translated into real public policy in the bureaucracy. The fourteen cabinet departments and fifty-seven independent agencies or government corporations make important policy decisions affecting millions. As the role of the national government has expanded, the national legislature and executive have increasingly delegated authority to administrative agencies to make fundamental policy decisions. These agencies make important decisions, such as whether RU-486 should be available to American women, whether race-based educational and employment practices are permissible, and what levels of sulfur dioxide are permissible from smokestacks. Their decisions are published in the seventy thousand to eighty thousand pages of the *Federal Register*, and they represent to many citizens the exercise of public authority. For many people, their only concrete experience with the national government is their contact with an administrative agency like the Social Security Administration, the Immigration and Naturalization Service, or the Internal Revenue Service.

How this administrative state is designed, its coherence, its responsiveness, and its efficacy determine, in Robert Dahl's phrase, "who gets what, when, and how." From direct income transfers like social security to less direct policies with redistributive consequences like environmental regulations, the assignment of broadcasting frequencies, and law enforcement, the bureaucracy is the vehicle of public authority. Thus the study of the administrative state is extremely important for understanding American politics and policy. To comprehend how the administrative state works, we must first examine how agencies get created and designed. Before any appointee is nominated, before any executive order is issued, and before any budget is enacted, political actors have deliberated over, bargained about, and struggled for specific agency designs.

Given the importance of the bureaucracy for making important public policy decisions, it should be no surprise that agency design is more the product of politics than of any rational or overarching plan for effective administration. Agency design is fundamentally and inescapably political. As Terry Moe (1989, 267) famously argued, "American public bureaucracy is not designed to be effective. The bureaucracy rises out of politics, and its design reflects the interests, strategies, and compromises of those who exercise political power." With the increasing importance of the bureaucracy as a creator and instigator of public policy, modern political actors recognize how important agency design is.

But the political nature of agency design goes deeper, rooted in the very Constitution that shapes the American governing system. The framers and ratifiers of the Constitution were more concerned with the abuse of government power and authority than with empowering an administrative state. They designed the constitutional system to restrict the use of power. They divided power among the branches and between the federal and state governments. They added the Bill of Rights to give individuals protections against the abuse of federal power. By neither describing nor empowering an administrative state, the Constitution's framers granted political actors in legislative and executive branches the power to create and design the administrative state based upon their own interests. Thus their actions guaranteed that the administrative state would be the product of interests shaped by the unique institutional perspective of each branch's occupants and their partisan disagreements.

WHY STUDY AGENCY DESIGN?

To understand agency design is to understand something fundamental about American politics, namely that forces set in motion at the nation's founding shape modern politics, modern choices, and modern political behavior. Embedded in American politics are perspectives and incentives shaped by constitutional institutions as they have been interpreted over time by the interaction of the three branches. Each branch is endowed with a perspective based upon a unique role in the American separation-of-powers system and a unique constitutionally shaped political constituency.

But understanding agency design also gives us insight into politics in its most basic form. If the Founders did not foresee that national decision making would be shaped by political opinion rather than high-minded political deliberation, political practitioners did. Their calculations about the "proper" design of administrative agencies are shaped less by concerns for efficiency or effectiveness than by concerns about reelection, political control, and, ultimately, policy outcomes. Their design decisions boil down to base calculations such as "Is someone who thinks like me going to be in control or someone with a different view?" and "What impact will the likely agency head have on policy?" They care more immediately about the policy consequences of their choices than about the aggregate coherence of the administrative state they are building.

A study of agency design tells us something fundamental about who will create and implement public policy, about power and who will exercise it. Agency design determines, among other things, the degree to which current and future political actors can change the direction of public policy by nonlegislative means. Some structural arrangements allow more control by political actors than others do. Agencies like the independent regulatory commissions, for example, are insulated from political control by commission structures that dilute political accountability, party-balancing requirements that diminish the impact of changing administrations, and fixed terms for commissioners that limit the influence of any one administration on commission policy. If we want to understand why bureaucracy is too "politicized" or, conversely, pathologically unresponsive, the appropriate place to begin is the start: the choice of administrative structure.

Presidents and Public Accountability

Agency design determines bureaucratic responsiveness to democratic impulses and pressure, particularly those channeled through elected officials like the president. It can determine the success or failure of modern presidents in meeting constitutional and electoral mandates. One of the central concerns of presidency scholars beginning with Richard Neustadt (1960) has been increasing public expectations of presidents (Lowi 1985; Skowronek 1993). The president is held accountable for the success or failure of the entire government. When the economy is in recession, when an agency blunders, or when some social problem goes unaddressed, it is the president whose reelection and historical legacy are on the line (Moe and Wilson 1994). Presidents have responded to these increased expectations in a number of ways, including increased public activities, the development of the Executive Office of the President, and attempts to politicize the bureaucracy and centralize its control in the White House. With so much policy-making authority delegated to executive branch actors, coupled with the difficulty of legislative action during a period largely characterized by divided government, presidents have powerful incentives to influence policy administratively (Nathan 1975, 1983).

Presidents seek control of the bureaucracy not only to influence public policy and meet public expectations but also because presidents are held accountable for their performance as managers. The chief executive is charged with the responsibility to see that the law is "faithfully executed" and is held accountable electorally. As such, presidents care about government structure and responsiveness. Every modern president has attempted to reshape the bureaucracy by eliminating overlapping jurisdictions, duplication of administrative functions, and fragmented political control (Arnold 1998; Emmerich 1971). Modern presidents have also sought to increase their institutional resources to facilitate this control (Burke 1992). Agencies that are insulated from their control, and the increasing bureaucratic fragmentation that results from that insulation, significantly constrain the president's ability to manage the bureaucracy and satisfy public expectations.

For example, one way agency design influences the ability of presidents

Choice of Institutional Structure
Governance by board or administrator?
Which positions require confirmation?
Fixed, staggered terms?
Limitations on appointments?
Limitations on removal?

The Appointment
Who gets appointed—party, ideology, region, race, senatorial courtesy?
Who has influence—interests, executive, Senate?
How are they appointed?—regular, recess?
How long did it take?

Impact of Appointment on Policy
Does appointment change agency policy?
Does appointee exercise influence?
Does appointment change inputs, outputs?

FIGURE 0.1   Three Sets of Research Questions

to control the administrative state is through political appointments. But we know very little about this part of the appointments process. Broadly conceived, there are three sets of research questions on administrative appointments (see Figure 0.1). The first is the design and institutional structure of administrative agencies. Each agency is designed differently, and an agency's distinctive characteristics shape the appointment process in underappreciated ways. For example, boards or commissions govern some administrative agencies, whereas administrators govern others. The appointment of some administrative officials with commensurate responsibilities requires Senate confirmation, whereas others do not. Some political appointees serve fixed terms, and others serve at the pleasure of the president. Limitations, based on background or political party, are sometimes placed on the types of persons that may be appointed.

Introduction

The second set of questions is about the appointment itself. A great deal of past work explains the motivations of presidents, legislators, and interest groups in the appointment process. From the presidential perspective, some of these works explain presidential goals and strategies in the nomination of public officials (Mackenzie 1981; Moe 1985). Other works focus on the confirmation of nominees in the Senate by examining legislative preferences and appointment outcomes (see, e.g., Segal, Cameron, and Cover 1992). In general, research in this area examines the approval or rejection of some appointees, the varying confirmation times, and the appointment of some types of individuals rather than others.

The final set of questions concerns the impact of a political appointment on policy outcomes. Past research in this area explains how political appointments affect administrative policy (Clayton 1992; Moe 1982; Randall 1979; Stewart and Cromartie 1982; Wood 1990; Wood and Anderson 1993; Wood and Waterman 1991, 1994). It explains how political appointees differ from civil servants and the difficulty political appointees have in orchestrating policy change (Downs 1967).

An extensive appointments literature connects the choice of appointments to policy outcomes. However, this research fails to recognize that the choice of institutional structures, which occurs prior to appointment, has a large impact on both the choice of appointments and policy outcomes. Because political actors choose structure carefully, with the intention of shaping both the appointment and policy-making process (Horn 1995; McCarty 1999; McCubbins, Noll and Weingast 1989; Moe 1989, 1990b; Moe and Wilson 1994), we cannot understand appointments and administrative policy making without understanding how the original institutional choices shape, constrain, and direct the politics of appointments and policy outcomes. As Richard Waterman (1989, 40) argues, "Organizational structure is not neutral. The manner in which an agency or department is organized can have a major impact on policy outcomes."

Agency Design and Bureaucratic Effectiveness

By allowing political actors in Congress and the presidency to jointly create the administrative state, the Constitution's framers guaranteed that agencies would be created more directly in response to political considerations than any notion of effectiveness. This is not to suggest that political actors care nothing about effectiveness. Rather it is to suggest that if effectiveness is not the primary goal, it will probably not be the primary outcome. If we want to understand the pathologies of the modern administrative state, we must understand the politics of its creation.

In 1936, President Franklin Delano Roosevelt appointed a commission of academics to study organizational problems in the executive branch. Part of Roosevelt's response to the Depression had been to convince Congress to pass a substantial amount of New Deal legislation. Along with this new authority, Roosevelt advocated the creation of scores of new administrative agencies to implement it.[1] Some of these agencies were standard bureaus placed within the existing cabinet structure. A significant portion of the New Deal bureaucracy, however, was created outside the normal cabinet structure to remove it from what Roosevelt perceived as the conservative bias in the bureaucracy. Many of the new agencies were designed as commissions or hybrid agencies like government corporations. The admittedly dramatic and haphazard expansion of the administrative state led Roosevelt to acknowledge in 1936 that some study of executive administration would be helpful.

One of the conclusions of the President's Committee on Administrative Management (1937), as it was called, was that "the Executive Branch . . . has . . . grown up without a plan or design like the barns, shacks, silos, tool sheds, and garages of an old farm." The implication of this conclusion was that the ramshackle nature of agency creation had led to organization problems and fragmentation of control.

Organization Problems

It is somewhat controversial in modern public administration to argue that duplication and overlapping responsibilities are necessarily bad. Indeed, some amount of redundancy and duplication can be desirable in large organizations in order to take "auxiliary precautions" in case some important bureaucratic process breaks down or to induce competition among agencies that will improve performance among all.[2] Yet what is equally true is that agencies that are not designed to be effective probably will not be, and most of the duplication, fragmentation, and overlap in the administrative state is not purposefully chosen to take auxiliary precautions or improve effectiveness via competition. It is chosen most immediately to remove certain policies from presidential political influence.

When agencies are most directly created in response to political concerns, organization problems naturally follow in the executive branch because of overlapping missions, conflicting goals, or unclear jurisdictions.[3] Agencies created under such conditions are more likely to have missions similar to those of other agencies. By the time of the Johnson administration, Senator Abraham Ribicoff (D-Conn.) counted 150 federal agencies providing aid to cities, states, and individuals through 456 different programs. There are four different government agencies regulating banking activity: the Office of the Comptroller of the Currency, the Office of Thrift Supervision, the Federal Reserve, and the Federal Deposit Insurance Corporation. There are at least twelve federal agencies that govern food safety and inspection.[4]

Agencies created most directly in response to political concerns also are more likely to have conflicting missions. For example, the Department of Agriculture is responsible both for promoting farming and for regulating farmers' practices with regard to the environment. Finally, agencies created in response to these pressures are more likely to suffer from unclear jurisdictions. As Amy Beth Zegart (1999) points out, multiple agencies engage in intelligence gathering, including the Central Intelligence Agency (CIA), the Federal Bureau of Investigation, and the Defense Intelligence Agency, and the unique politics at the time of the CIA's creation partly led to this outcome.

Of course, politics or not, some of these problems are unavoidable. Some coordination problems arise because some agencies are purpose-based and some are client-based. There will be natural tension, for example, between the health functions of the Department of Health and Human Services and those of the Department of Veterans Affairs or the Bureau of Indian Affairs that can lead to inefficiency and duplication. Agencies also change their missions. For example, the national weapons labs like Lawrence Livermore National Laboratory and Los Alamos National Laboratory have become competitors with federal government science agencies for biological, environmental science, nanotechnology, and geological research money. In addition, it would be impossible to differentiate mutually exclusive spheres of government activity and design the administrative state entirely along functional lines. Some duplication, confusion, and overlap is unavoidable.[5]

When agencies grow up "like the barns, shacks, silos, tool sheds, and garages of an old farm," however, inefficiencies will result. Political actors can come back later with plans for horizontal coordination through inter-agency committees, vertical coordination through czar-type positions, or reorganization, but the need for these types of remedies demonstrates the impact that agency design can have on the functioning of the executive branch. Indeed, part of the reason Congress has been convinced at different points in time to appoint study commissions on executive branch organization, grant reorganization authority to presidents, and pass legislation to remedy agency design problems is legislators' own recognition that the natural agency design impulses of our system can lead to perverse outcomes in the aggregate.

Political Insulation and Fragmentation of Control

One of the main sources of administrative diversity and fragmentation is attempts by political actors to insulate new administrative agencies from political control. Politicians seek policy gains that endure. They seek to ensure that the authority they delegate to bureaucrats will result in the types of public policy outputs they prefer both now and in the future. They know that all statutory language contains some ambiguity, and political appointees can use this ambiguity and discretion to move policy away from the preferences of its principal supporters. Electoral turnover can also threaten the durability of new policies.

One means of ensuring a specific outcome is to protect bureaucrats from political pressure to change policies both now and in the future. There are many different ways that politicians insulate policies they care about. One of the most prominent means is to write very specific statutes (Epstein and O'Halloran 1999; Horn 1995; Moe 1989). Specific statutes remove administrative discretion and limit the degree to which administrative actors can alter policy without passing new legislation. Political actors also insulate policies through different budgetary devices such as automatic cost-of-living increases, permanent budget authorization, or restrictive appropriations language.

Administrative procedures are another means of protecting specific policy outcomes. They can be designed to require notification of and participation by key interests in any agency rule making, thereby ensuring an outcome acceptable to the groups Congress is trying to satisfy (McCubbins, Noll, and Weingast 1987, 1989; McCubbins and Schwartz 1984). The final,

9

and perhaps most important, means of insulating certain policies from political influence is to design new administrative agencies with characteristics that insulate them from political control. Some structural arrangements allow more control by political actors than others.[6]

Each of these forms of insulation contributes to the fragmentation and administrative incoherence of the bureaucracy. An abundance of specific statutes can remove the administrative discretion necessary for the effective implementation of complex public policies (see, e.g., Derthick 1990; Moe 1989). In 1970, for example, William Ruckelshaus, the first administrator of the Environmental Protection Agency (EPA), was given only sixty days to change the emissions behavior of the entire United States automotive industry to comply with the Clean Air Act and other environmental legislation. Legislators, dissatisfied with the perceived indifference of the Nixon administration to environmental concerns, wrote very specific requirements into environmental legislation to ensure that the EPA acted in a manner consistent with the intent of the environmental majority in Congress.

Budget devices to insulate policies also remove administrative discretion. Mandatory spending accounts and entitlements that are automatically increased to track with inflation are the fastest-growing portion of the U.S. budget. These accounts bypass review by appropriations committees and account for about 65 percent of the federal budget. Policy makers do not review them like other appropriations requests and cannot adjust them to accommodate other administrative needs without writing new legislation.

The Administrative Procedures Act of 1946 and subsequent amendments to it require that agencies give notice, issue comments, allow participation by relevant parties, and consider evidence before issuing new rules. Notification, participation, and evidentiary requirements slow down administrative decision making. They also decrease administrative discretion since they allow time for the mobilization and participation of groups in the decision-making process. Dissatisfied groups can also ask for help from sympathetic members of Congress if they are adversely affected by agency decisions.

The design of administrative agencies to be removed from political control is the most conspicuous and perhaps most pernicious source of fragmentation and administrative incoherence. Every commission on the organization and efficiency of the executive branch in the twentieth century has lamented the increasing number of administrative agencies placed outside of the traditional hierarchical structure of the cabinet departments.[7] The President's Committee on Administrative Management (1937, 3) stated, "The Whole Executive Branch of the Government should be overhauled and the present 100 agencies reorganized under a few large departments in which every executive activity would find its place." Of particular concern to the commission was the increasing number of agencies created outside the cabinet departments, particularly those insulated from presidential direction.

If the natural agency design process of the federal government leads to a decrease in the president's ability to meet public expectations and an increase in organization problems and bureaucratic fragmentation, why do political actors persist in creating insulated agencies? The answer is they cannot help it. The design process is fundamentally the product of institutional incentives. At points, Congress has recognized the aggregate consequences of its agency design choices and has acceded to or explicitly approved study commissions like the Brownlow Committee, the two Hoover Commissions, the Ash Council, and the National Performance Review. Congress has also seen fit to grant reorganization authority to the president or his subordinates. In individual cases, however, the product of congressional incentives and compromises are agency designs that create organization problems and fragmentation of control in the aggregate.

WHAT DO WE KNOW ABOUT AGENCY DESIGN?

Unfortunately, agency design historically has received little direct attention from scholars in American politics. Indeed, students and scholars alike are often surprised to hear that agencies are not designed according to some rational plan. Many frequently note the difficulty in discerning regular patterns or developing theories of agency design. William Fox (1997), for example, argues that "there is little rhyme or reason as to Congress' designation of a particular agency as either a cabinet agency or an independent regulatory commission." He concludes that "political motivations" best explain the choice of organizational structure. Harold Seidman (1998, 161) states: "The interplay of competing and often contradictory political, economic, social, and regional forces within our constitutional system and pluralistic society has produced a smorgasbord of institutional types. . . . Choices are influenced by a complex tangle of tangible and intangible factors." Indeed, most accounts of agency design focus on the idiosyncratic politics of each individual case rather than recurring patterns across time (see, e.g., Cushman 1972; Rourke 1957).

Other attempts to systematically explain variation among types of agencies hypothesize that what agencies do determines their structure. Yet no federal law mandates the appropriate organizational form for different types of government activity. For example, although considerable regulatory authority is granted to independent regulatory commissions like the Federal Communications Commission, the Federal Trade Commission, or the Securities and Exchange Commission, an equal amount is granted to more traditional hierarchical structures like the Food and Drug Administration in the U.S. Department of Health and Human Services and the Environmental Protection Agency. Even adjudicatory functions are handled in a variety of different structural types from administrative law judges within cabinet departments to independent commissions like the War Claims Commission. Sales-financed government activity is not necessarily the province of government corporations. Responsibility for the liquidation of government assets, a clear example of such activity, has been lodged to cabinet departments, independent commissions, or government corporations.

The New Economics of Organization

Scholars employing new theoretical tools under the rubric of the "New Economics of Organization" (NEO) have begun to shed some light on the agency design choice mainly through their analyses of congressional delegation decisions. The approach has been somewhat different. Using the tools of principal-agent theory and transaction cost economics, these scholars have sought explicitly to build theories by stripping away some of the complexity of individual decisions. By focusing on regular patterns over time and abstracting from the idiosyncrasies of individual cases, their hope is to build theories that explain most of the variance in individual delegation and design decisions.[8]

The bulk of this work looks at agency design only indirectly, through a focus on congressional delegation. It has focused on attempts by legislators under different strategic constraints to reduce the costs of getting agencies to implement the policies they prefer. They key problem for political actors is to benefit from the expertise of bureaucrats by giving them discretion yet still ensuring that the authority they delegate is used properly. Variance in policy preferences, the degree of uncertainty, and institutional perspective shape the eventual decision. In this view, if we understand the incentives of the actors, their policy preferences, and the degree of uncertainty, we can predict what decisions will be.

Morris Fiorina (1986), for example, argues that the policy preferences of individual legislators coupled with legislative uncertainty over the implementation of policy determines the preferences of legislators for different administrative enforcement mechanisms. Mathew McCubbins (1985) suggests that uncertainty and conflict among legislators affect the choice of procedural constraints on administrative agencies. McCubbins, Roger Noll, and Barry Weingast (1987, 1989) argue that administrative design can be a means of resolving problems associated with the principal-agent relationship that exists between political actors and the bureaucracy.

Moe (1989) argues that disagreements over policy, unique perspectives based upon constitutional role, and uncertainty about future political control shape the agency design decision.[9] Murray Horn (1995) argues that different configurations of transaction costs associated with different types of policy (e.g., regulation, production, sales) affect the preferences of legislative coalitions for different types of administrative structures.[10] David Epstein and Sharyn O'Halloran (1999) argue that the degree of authority delegated, the extent of procedural constraints placed upon the exercise of this authority, and the instrument employed to implement this delegated authority are chosen to minimize the transaction costs of the median legislator. These transaction costs vary based upon the complexity of the issue involved, the preferences of the president, and the uncertainty of outcomes.

The NEO approach has identified some of the crucial factors in the agency design decision. In particular, it has highlighted the role that institutions play in shaping decisions about the administrative state. The separation-of-powers system in the United States, which partly separates policy formation and execution, creates unique problems for political actors. It also creates different perspectives on agency design depending upon where you sit in the process. The political nature of the agency design decision also is emphasized. Actors with different policy preferences disagree about agency design because they worry about the influence of their opponents on the agency.

Limitations of Early NEO Research

Although these NEO approaches have added valuable new insight, they
have rarely addressed agency design directly.[11] They focus, instead, on delegation and, as such, there exists a bias in the literature toward the role and
power of Congress to the detriment of the fair presentation of presidential
incentives and power in the agency design process. Delegation, not design,
was the crucial decision for Congress scholars. Agency design was only one
of several means of ensuring that delegated authority was used consistently
with congressional preferences. This methodological bias toward Congress
led some to assume that Congress dominates the politics of agency creation, ignoring the unique institution-created incentives that differentiate
the president's perspective from that of members of Congress.

Presidents are, for all intents and purposes, left out. McCubbins, Noll,
and Weingast (1987, 1989), for example, argue that administrative design
can be a means of resolving problems associated with the principal-agent
relationship that exists between political actors and the bureaucracy. Their
discussion, however, focuses mainly on the principal-agent relationship between Congress and the bureaucracy. Presidents, when included, are characterized as part of an enacting coalition who have preferences over structure similar to those of legislators. Horn (1995) attempts to explain variation
in bureaucratic structure as an attempt by legislators to reduce different
types of transaction costs. He assumes for simplicity that presidents are part
of the enacting coalition. In Epstein and O'Halloran's (1999) model the
president is important only to the extent the he can appoint executive officials, influencing the calculation of the median legislator about how much
discretion a new agency should have. The president has no direct role in institutional design (see also Bawn 1995, 1997; Epstein and O'Halloran 1994,
1996; Fiorina 1986; Macey 1992; McCubbins 1985).

Moe (1989, 1990a, 1990b) and Moe and Scott Wilson (1994) articulate an
important exception to this line of research. Moe argues that administrative
design is the result of a bargain between the president and Congress and
cannot be understood without a proper understanding of the influence of
presidents. Presidents benefit from their legislative role and the administrative discretion arising from Congress's imperfect ability to control executive branch creation of administrative agencies.

Presidents generally oppose attempts to insulate. They are held accountable for the successes and failures of the entire government, and attempts to insulate not only limit their ability to achieve policy goals through the administration but also hinder their ability to manage the bureaucracy. As a consequence, they consistently oppose attempts to insulate using their broad formal and informal powers. The president takes advantage of collective action problems in Congress, unilaterally creates agencies that are not insulated, and uses other formal powers to persuade Congress to do likewise.[12]

But Moe's work has its own difficulties. One of the early tasks of NEO scholars was to prove that things like agency design were political at all. Moe (1989) tackled this question directly by presenting a theory of agency design and illustrating that agency design could be political with three case studies. Although Moe's work does show agency design to be political and does present a more interinstitutional theory of agency design, parts remain unclear and difficult to test, including the role of political compromise and how the different forms of "insulation" relate.[13]

There is confusion about when we should expect political actors to create "insulated" political structures like the Consumer Product Safety Commission and when we should expect political actors to design run-of-the-mill bureaus. Where does the variance in agency design come from? Moe characterizes presidential preferences over structure as constant. Presidents always oppose demands for insulation. Such demands must then come from interest groups and the legislators that parrot their concerns. But Moe's characterization of Congress and interest groups always includes majorities and their opponents, and he argues that outcomes are fundamentally the product of compromise between an agency's proponents and opponents. Do we assume that it is the strength of the proponents vis-à-vis the opponents that determines the outcome? If so, a difficulty arises in disentangling uncertainty and coalition strength. Uncertainty and coalition strength are interrelated. The more uncertain a coalition is, the weaker it is, and the more likely it is that it will have to compromise with its opponents. Uncertainty leads the coalition to want to insulate, but its lack of strength means it will be unable to. Hence, no clear prediction follows from Moe's theory. It suggests both insulation and no insulation. Progress requires more determinate predictions.

Finally, Moe does not sufficiently disentangle different strategies for removing agencies from political control. Different actions taken by political actors have differential effects on political actors. It is therefore necessary in a theory of agency design to specify the form of insulation and who is harmed. Presidents, for example, likely do not mind Congress giving up control of agencies by lengthening the sunset on authorization legislation or giving presidents agenda control over agency design through reorganization legislation. They oppose vehemently, however, attempts to give appointees fixed terms or impose party-balancing limitations on appointments.

A FRESH LOOK THEORETICALLY AND EMPIRICALLY

The task for this book, then, is to build on the insights of the early NEO literature to present an explanation of agency design in modern American politics that can be tested with data from the post–World War II period. I build on Moe's insights about how our separation-of-powers system creates unique incentives for presidents in the agency design process. Presidents view design of the administrative state from their vantage point as chief executive and the nation's only nationally elected political official (along with the vice president). Members of Congress care less holistically about the design of the administrative state. They are more attuned to the short-term parochial interests that are key to their reelection. I also explain how the president's advantages as a unitary versus collective actor influence agency design.

I use the delegation literature's insights about congressional decision making to suggest when members will seek to remove agencies from political control. Members fundamentally seek to limit the president when the president is likely to exert influence over the agency in a way inconsistent with their preferences either now or in the future. However, their ability to overcome collective action problems and come to agreement is a key factor in determining agency design outcomes.

This book presents a more complete and testable theory of the agency design process. It incorporates theoretical insights about differing institutional perspectives, policy differences, and temporal considerations and abstracts from the idiosyncrasies of individual cases into a larger theory of agency design. The theory presents a more accurate picture of the president's role in the agency design process.

This theory of agency design is tested with two case studies and quantitative data collected on administrative agencies created in the United States between 1946 and 1997. These are the first quantitative data on agency design. As such, they provide a unique opportunity not only to describe the existing design of United States government bureaucracy but also to test applicability of the theory with quantitative data.

What Is Omitted?

Like earlier NEO scholars, I do not look at everything. I must leave out some aspects of the agency design decision that may also be important. First, for simplicity, I examine structural choices only, particularly five structural choices that insulate new agencies from presidential control. I do not examine the creation of administrative procedures, the specificity of statutes, or budgetary devices meant to constrain administrative officials. Although the discussion of separation of powers and policy interests has broad applicability to the politics of delegation and the choice of other means of *ex ante* control, and these characteristics are sometimes discussed, the main focus of the work is on structural choices at the moment of agency creation.

Second, I assume for the sake of simplicity that a fixed amount of authority has already been delegated at the point of decision about agency design. The omission of the delegation decision is necessary for a couple of reasons. First, it allows us to focus more specifically on the agency design choice. By doing so, we can ultimately understand the delegation decision better. Second, it makes sense because agency design decisions are frequently divorced from the initial delegation decision, particularly in cases of administrative creation. Administrative agencies are rarely created new out of whole cloth, regardless of size, function, or origination. New agencies invariably combine existing personnel, resources, appropriations, and delegated functions into a new administrative unit. As such, it makes good sense to separate agency design from the initial delegation decision.

I self-consciously omit some factors that might influence the agency design decision. In particular I omit extensive discussion of interest groups and bureaucratic actors, both because of existing research highlighting some of their influence and because it makes the most sense to focus on the political actors in the political system that have the most proximate impact on the agency design decision.[14]

Simplification purchases the ability to illuminate a critical part of American politics. It reveals the fundamental logic undergirding the modern politics of agency design and reinforces our understanding that agency design and creation constitute a political choice. This choice is shaped by policy preferences at the time of agency creation filtered through the institutions of our separation-of-powers system. It reinforces our belief in a strong and independent executive who brings both a unique perspective and formidable powers to negotiations over the design of the administrative state. Through the process of this study, we can gain new insight into modern American public policy making, presidential control of the bureaucracy, and difficulties modern presidents face in meeting public expectations for the deliverance of public goods and public policy outputs.

PLAN OF THE BOOK

In Chapter 1 I explain how the separation of powers shapes the agency design process. I examine how presidents and members of Congress view the process differently, based upon their unique, institution-created perspectives. Modern presidents take a larger view based upon their position as chief executive and their national election constituency. Members of Congress make decisions about agency design on more proximate concerns tied to reelection interests, not an aggregate picture of administrative rationality. The bureaucracy reflects the agreements, disagreements, and negotiations of the branches over time subject to the constraints of the courts and the Constitution. I also explain how partisan politics plays a role in agency design. When Congress shares the president's policy preferences, it helps presidents create agencies with substantial executive influence. Even in cases where substantial opposition to the president exists in Congress, presidents can prevail. When Congress lacks the capacity to overcome presidential opposition, presidents are more likely to get the types of agencies they prefer. I summarize the conclusions of the chapter into a series of propositions and translate these propositions into predictions about divided government and party size in Congress.

In Chapter 2 I test the theory of agency design presented in Chapter 1. I describe quantitative data I collected on agencies created in the United States between 1946 and 1997. The chapter describes how politicians design agencies to be insulated from presidential control, focusing on agency location, independence, governance by commission, fixed terms for appointees, and specific qualifications for political appointees. I examine the number of new agencies created with different insulating characteristics over time and then move to estimation of econometric models. These models test whether the propositions identified in Chapter 1 are confirmed by the data.

In Chapter 3 I return to explaining the design of administrative agencies. I examine how presidents influence the design of administrative agencies and argue that models of the political insulation process that omit the president overestimate the influence of Congress in the process. I argue that presidents have distinct, institution-driven incentives to oppose insulation in new administrative agencies. They exercise influence in both the legislative process and through administrative action. The chapter describes how presidents translate their legislative power of the veto, their position as chief executive, and their position as a unitary actor into influence in Congress. It also describes how presidents create administrative agencies through executive action.

In Chapter 4 I examine the agencies created by executive action: executive orders, departmental orders, and reorganization plans. I show that agencies created by administrative action are much less likely to be insulated than other agencies. Through a case study of the National Biological Service and quantitative analysis of count data from 1946 to 1997, I show that presidents have more discretion when Congress cannot act. Not only are agencies created by executive action less likely to be insulated, but more are created during periods when the congressional majority is weak, implying that presidents use the weakness of Congress to get the types of agencies they prefer.

In Chapter 5 I revisit the analysis in Chapter 2 to show that presidents have tremendous influence in the design of administrative agencies. I present a case study of the creation of the National Nuclear Security Agency, a case in which the president arguably lost out in his struggle with Congress, to illustrate just how much influence presidents have. I then revisit the quantitative analysis from Chapter 2 with an eye toward testing for the influence of presidents. The chapter shows that agencies created under strong presidents are less likely to be insulated than other agencies.

Chapter 6 addresses the question of whether or not agency insulation matters. It seeks to determine whether agencies that are insulated are more durable than other agencies. Since organizational change usually accompanies policy change, I analyze the rate of organizational change in administrative agencies to determine whether policies in insulated agencies are more likely to change than other policies. I demonstrate that agencies that are insulated from presidential influence are more likely to survive than other agencies and discuss the implications of this finding for the politics of agency design and presidential attempts to manage the executive branch.

In the final chapter I conclude that agency design is a political process but one that, properly studied, can be understood. I discuss several questions that are left unanswered by the analysis, including questions about the "proper" design of administrative agencies, the implications of the research for the New Economics of Organization, and what we should expect in the future.

(I)

Separation of Powers and the Design of Administrative Agencies

> There is no danger in power, if only it be not irresponsible. If it be divided, dealt only in shares to many, it is obscured; and if it be obscured, it is made irresponsible. But if it be centred in heads of the service and in heads of branches of the service, it is easily watched and brought to book.

—Woodrow Wilson, *The Study of Administration*

In 1938, Senator Harry S Truman (D-Mo.) argued that the Interstate Commerce Commission should regulate the nation's waterways in addition to its railways. Truman justified his proposal by arguing, "Transportation should be no political football" (*Cong. Rec.* 1937, 81, pt. 6:6745). Truman and his colleagues believed that placing authority for the regulation of waterways in a cabinet department would make it too susceptible to political interference, and they worried about the discontinuities in policy and implementation that would arise from changing administrations and, perhaps, changing majorities in Congress. As a consequence, they proposed taking regulatory power and placing it not in a cabinet department but in an independent regulatory commission. Truman believed that independent regulatory commissions were less susceptible to presidential interference than their cabinet counterparts.

In 1946, after Truman ascended to the White House, his enthusiasm for delegating authority to independent regulatory commissions had waned. Instead of delegating authority to independent regulatory commissions, Truman favored a new Department of Transportation. He recognized that delegating power to insulated agencies came at a cost. Increased delegation to the independent regulatory commissions left the nation's transportation policy fragmented and unresponsive to the needs of important segments of society.

Truman's actions illustrate how the design of administrative agencies is shaped by our separation-of-powers system. His changing opinion coincided with his move from one branch of the government to another. By constitutional design the two branches view agency design differently, one from the parochial perspective of narrow reelection interests and the other from a broader perspective derived from unique constitutional responsibilities and a national constituency. In order to delve more deeply into the politics of agency design, we need to examine how presidents and members of Congress view the process differently based upon their unique, institution-created perspectives.

DESIGNING THE ADMINISTRATIVE STATE

The Constitution neither describes nor empowers an administrative state. There are spotted references to "officers" and "departments" but no provision creating them or describing what they should look like. The Founders left to the politicians the responsibility for designing the machinery of government, both what it would do and how it would do it. It should be no surprise that agency design is not the product of a high-minded desire for efficiency or rational design. Rather, the design of the administrative state is fundamentally the product of inter- and intra-branch negotiations among political actors with individual interests shaped both by the institutional incentives of their branches and by their policy preferences.

Although the legislative and executive branches share responsibility for designing the administrative state, most administrative law scholars believe that the bulk of the authority for agency design ultimately resides in Congress (see, e.g., Fox 1997; Gellhorn 1987). Congress is, after all, the lawmaking branch. Members of Congress, provided they can secure presidential agreement or override presidential opposition, can choose to design administrative agencies any way they desire, so long as they do not infringe on the president's own constitutional authority as chief executive.

It would be unprofitable and at some point unconstitutional, however, for

Congress to decide the design and functioning of the administrative state up to the minute detail. Although Congress has legitimate constitutional and political claims to run the executive branch, presidents and their subordinates also legitimately claim jurisdiction over how delegated authority will be executed—how many people are necessary, how they will be organized into an efficient organization, who will be hired, and what rules will govern their execution of legislatively granted authority. In some cases Congress has created new agencies and described them in great detail in statute. The principal offices are identified, rough guidelines are given about how many people will be hired, and an administrative structure is outlined.

In other cases, Congress simply grants new authority, responsibilities, and appropriations to the president or to the president's subordinates without directly addressing how the responsibilities will be implemented. Often there is embedded in legislation or congressional deliberation the implicit understanding that executive branch officials will do the designing and creation of the administrative units necessary to execute the federal government's new policies. In other cases, when Congress is silent, presidents use constitutional authority or vague delegations of authority to create agencies Congress did not necessarily anticipate and probably would not have created on its own. They take advantage of congressional inaction to secure the types of administrative structures they prefer.

The default administrative structure, and the one that dominated administrative design practices until the late 1800s, is the hierarchically organized bureau located squarely inside the cabinet structure, where presidents apoint a unitary director of their choosing and this officer serves at the president's pleasure. Ceteris paribus, these structures provide presidents more influence than do agencies with the insulating characteristics described in the introduction. Their heads serve at the pleasure of the president or the president's appointed subordinates. Responsibility is not diffused by a commission structure, and appointees are not protected by fixed terms or location outside the cabinet.

Congressional attempts to deviate from the bureau model generally arise from disagreements between members of Congress and the president. Some of these disagreements naturally arise from the *institutional* differences in the two branches. In Edward Corwin's famous phrase, the Constitution is an "invitation to struggle." The president and members of Congress view the administrative state from entirely different vantage points based upon their positions in the U.S. constitutional system, and these vantage points, along with their *policy preferences*, lead to disagreements about how the administrative state should be organized. Who ultimately prevails in these contests depends upon the strength and cohesion of Congress and the president's ability to translate the legislative power of the veto, the position as chief executive, and the position as a unitary actor into influence in Congress.

INSTITUTIONAL DIFFERENCES IN THE DESIGN OF THE ADMINISTRATIVE STATE

The Constitution states that the "executive power shall be vested in a president of the United States." It is not clear in the Constitution what exactly the Founders meant by executive power. They granted presidents the ability to secure in writing the recommendations of their principal officers, the ability to nominate principal officers, and the responsibility to faithfully execute the law. The reasonable interpretation of this grouping of powers, and one generally adopted by presidents, is that presidents are obligated to direct the executive branch of the government. In order for presidents to successfully carry out their oath of office, it is their responsibility to make sure the policies of the U.S. government are implemented effectively. To do so, they need control of the administrative apparatus of government. In short, they need the types of administrative structures that maximize presidential control, and the bureau model fits the bill.

The modern president's desire to control the bureaucracy is reinforced by electoral pressures. With the democratization of party nominating processes and the popular election of electors, presidents in the modern period are selected in what amounts to a national plebiscite. The president and vice president are the nation's only nationally elected political officials. This gives presidents a unique vantage point in our constitutional system.

With a large national constituency presidents are sensitive to those issues affecting the nation as a whole. Presidents are held accountable for the functioning of the entire government. When the economy is in recession, when an agency blunders, or when some social problem goes unaddressed, the president is the only public official voters can hold directly responsible

(Moe and Wilson 1994). Presidents cannot escape their responsibility to focus on those issues that affect the nation as a whole, such as various public goods like the economy, foreign affairs, and the performance of the administrative state.

In contrast, members of Congress represent individual districts or states, and their perspective derives from a constitutionally parochial view. They are elected to ensure the well-being of their constituency—nothing more, nothing less. To show that they are doing a good job and deserve to be returned to office, they must point to tangible benefits voters have received for having them in office. It is easier for members to point to particularistic benefits for which they can more credibly claim credit than to the provision of public goods. A voter's representative or senator is only one person in a large legislature, jointly responsible for the state of the nation. In many cases a legislator can point to specific cases where he or she tried to improve the state of the nation but were rebuffed by other members. Introducing legislation, cosponsoring legislation, and making public statements is costless activity that can give the impression that individual members are working hard to improve an obstinate Congress.

The difference in perspectives is reflected in the extent to which the twentieth-century Congress has delegated increasing amounts of authority to the president, both in general and specifically related to the provision of public goods. The result of this delegation has been not only increased authority for the president in providing public goods but also increased expectations of presidential behavior in these areas. Congress delegated significant economic policy-making responsibility through acts such as the Budget and Accounting Act of 1921, the Employment Act of 1946, and the Taft-Hartley Act of 1947. Similarly, decision making on the public goods components of foreign policy and defense has been shifting from the halls of Congress to the executive branch, as evidenced by the free hand presidents have had in committing troops, entering international agreements, and setting foreign policy. Of course, Congress has attempted to reestablish some control over economic policy in such cases as the Budget and Accounting Act of 1974 and the Budget Enforcement Act of 1990 and foreign policy in the Case Act, the War Powers Act, and the Boland Amendment. But delegation once given is hard to take back. Congress has given presidents enough of a role that it felt obligated to give presidents the administrative machinery to take the lead in these areas through the creation of the Bureau of the Budget / Office of Management and Budget, the Council of Economic Advisers, and the National Security Council.

The dramatic increase in both delegation of policy-making authority to the executive branch and expectations of presidential provision of policy goods has increased the stakes in the struggle over control of the executive branch. Presidents are both held accountable for the functioning of the entire bureaucracy as a public good and held accountable for the provision of policies that increasingly may be provided only through executive branch policy making. It is absolutely essential to modern presidents to have control over the executive branch. Modern presidency scholars have noted how presidents have centralized control over appointments in the White House (Weko 1995), used an appointments strategy for policy change (Nathan 1983), and increasingly used loyalty predominantly in picking nominees for administration posts (Moe 1985). Presidents have also sought additional control over the administrative state through reorganization (Benze 1985; Arnold 1998), through the budget (Canes-Wrone 1999), and through the centralization of administrative decision making in the Executive Office of the President. The success or failure of each of these strategies agency by agency and in the administrative state as a whole depends fundamentally, however, on the design of agencies. If agencies are insulated from presidential control, either by design or because they were designed without sufficient reference to existing administrative structures, presidential politicization and centralization of the bureaucracy will be of little use.

As a consequence, all modern presidents have attempted to prevent control problems by opposing agency designs that will limit their control or confuse lines of accountability. Historically, in the process of agency design and bureaucratic reorganization, presidents have focused on eliminating overlapping jurisdictions, duplication of administrative functions, and limits to their control. Presidents have also sought to increase their institutional resources in an effort to make the bureaucracy more manageable (Burke 1992).

What exactly does "manageable" mean, however? Presidents seek what Moe (1985, 239) calls "responsive competence" from the bureaucracy. They seek an administration that is capable, flexible, and responsive to the president, not insulated from their control. In practice, this has meant that presidents try to decrease their "span of control" or the number of agencies that report directly to the president. As the report of the President's Committee on Administrative Management (1937, 34) states, "Just as the hand can cover but a few keys on the piano, so there is for management a limited span of control." President Truman (1946, 1:292–94) stated in opposition to the creation of an independent Mediation Board, "Surely functions of this kind should be concentrated in the Department of Labor," and he reiterated his support for reorganization of government "into the fewest number of government agencies consistent with efficiency." President Nixon's Advisory Council on Executive Organization (1972, 50) listed as one of its main recommendations to reduce the total number of departments, thus reducing the president's span of control.

Presidents also want to be able to appoint officials to head administrative agencies that are responsive to executive direction and able to direct the agencies and offices below them. As a consequence, presidents prefer new agencies to be placed within existing hierarchically structured bureaucracies and headed by political appointees (Moe 1989; Seidman 1998). The first Hoover Commission recommended, for example, not only to regroup the sixty-five departments and agencies into a number one-third that size but also to limit the independent authority of subordinate officials (Emmerich 1971, 89).

But Congress, too, recognizes that the executive branch is an increasingly important location of policy making, and as such, members care about agency design, but they care in a different way than presidents do. Members of Congress are not institutionally situated to think about the administrative state as a whole when making agency design decisions. Congressional evaluation of whether or not a president should have more or less control depends upon the members' own assessment of how this will achieve their goals. Members of Congress do not garner reelection by providing public goods like a well-organized and effective administrative state. Instead, they receive more tangible reelection benefits by designing administrative agencies in response to key reelection interests, regardless of the aggregate consequences of such actions. They are content to give away presidential control and the benefits it provides in individual cases without reference to the long-term consequences of their actions.

Members of Congress know that policy outcomes depend not only on legislation passed in Congress but also on decisions made later. Appointments, executive directives, and budgets can all have a dramatic impact on the policy outputs after legislation has been enacted. In response, Congress, at times, tries to circumscribe the president's influence with commissions instead of administrations, fixed terms for appointees, qualifications for appointees, and location outside the cabinet.

Congress historically has only done so occasionally. If Congress and the president jointly share responsibility for overseeing the bureaucracy and important public policy decisions are made in the bureaucracy, Congress should want more control relative to the president. Why does Congress not create agencies insulated from presidential control all the time? One reason is that the aggregate consequences of individual congressional design choices can be detrimental to congressional goals. Even Congress occasionally acknowledges that a fragmented and uncoordinated bureaucracy is ultimately counterproductive. Congressional support for unifying homeland security functions into one agency after the September 11 terrorist attacks is a good example (Peters 2001). Having homeland security functions dispersed throughout forty different federal agencies made the administration's task of responding to present attacks and preparing for future attacks more difficult. Similarly, food safety advocates' recent push for a unified food safety agency was sparked, in part, by inefficiencies in the current food safety regime (Freedman 1998a, 1998b). These inefficiencies are partly due to the dispersal of authority to four different federal agencies.

But the question goes deeper than this. Members of Congress accept in principle that the natural agency design impulses coming from Congress— to remove agencies from presidential control in response to particularistic influences—can lead to duplication, overlap, unclear lines of authority, and losses of efficiency in the long run. They recognize that presidential coordination, centralization, and management provide some benefit and are at least partly beneficial for effective governance. This is part of the reason why they have been convinced at different points in time to appoint study commissions on executive branch organization, grant reorganization authority to presidents, and pass legislation that remedies their agency design excesses. In practice, in individual cases, however, they will give up the benefits of centralization and presidential control to satisfy reelection concerns.

A second reason why Congress does not always insulate agencies is that members of Congress sometimes prefer *more* presidential control when it will lead to more effective implementation of policies they care about. Insulation from presidential control comes at a cost. It decreases presidential control for both good and bad (Moe 1989). One of the frequent criticisms of the independent regulatory commissions, for example, is that their commission structure makes them unresponsive, slow, inefficient, and unable to plan (Bernstein 1977; Peterson 1985). Members of Congress give up the benefits of presidential coordination and direction when they insulate. They make a choice between administrative agencies that are effective and responsive to political direction but subject to policy change from electoral volatility and agencies that are a bit less effective and responsive to presidential direction but insulated from policy change stemming from party turnover in Congress and the presidency. The best of all worlds is an agency subject to hierarchical control by a political actor sympathetic to the preferred viewpoint. Short of that, political actors would rather create agencies to perform their desired mission and then remove them from the influence of political officials.

A final reason why Congress does not always insulate is that members of Congress could not circumscribe the president's authority all the time, even if they wanted to. Presidents oppose Congress's attempts to insulate, and Congress historically has not been successful in promoting its institutional interests vis-à-vis the president. Congress's ability to defend its institutional interests in agency design depends fundamentally on the distribution of preferences among members. Members who disagree fundamentally with the president and worry about future presidential influence over the agency support agency designs that lessen presidential influence, but members who share the president's policy goals prefer *more* presidential control. In the eyes of the latter group, presidents can appoint like-minded agency heads, provide necessary direction through executive directives, and propose adequate funding levels in future budgets. These actions will ensure a more effective implementation of the policy these members prefer.

To say that Congress has one institutional view is a mistake. There are always those who support less presidential control and those who support more. The key factor is whether those favoring less presidential control are strong enough to impose their will. As such, we need to explore how individual members of Congress make decisions about agency design and how preferences in Congress are aggregated. For presidents are most likely to get the types of structures they prefer when a significant number of members agree with their policy preferences or when enough members of Congress do not agree to overcome presidential opposition.

POLICY DIFFERENCES AND THE DESIGN OF THE ADMINISTRATIVE STATE

Congress members' calculation about whether or not to support an administrative design that insulates the agency and policy from presidential influence is not complicated. In the language of rational choice theory, there is both a spatial and a temporal component to their calculation. First, members evaluate the proximity of their policy preferences to those of the president and determine whether they are likely to agree or disagree with the direction the president will take the agency. Second, they try to determine what administrative influence the current president and future presidents will have on the policy Congress enacts, caring marginally more about the near future than the distant future.

When the president is unlikely to be supportive of policies supported by Congress members, they seek to insulate as much as possible from presidential control. The creation of the Consumer Product Safety Commission (CPSC) is a good example (see Moe 1989). In the early 1970s consumer groups had successfully pressured both the president and Congress for a new agency. In 1971, President Nixon proposed a new Consumer Safety Administration to be located in the Department of Health, Education, and Welfare. Proponents in Congress, however, worried about Nixon's ties to business interests, proposed an independent regulatory structure instead. The eventual CPSC was placed outside of existing bureaucratic structures and outfitted with a commission structure. To further insulate it from political manipulation, commissioners were granted seven-year terms. Since members in Congress will be more worried about the influence of the president during periods when their preferences diverge from those of presidents, they should attempt to insulate new agencies more frequently during these periods.

Proposition 1: Members of Congress are more likely to pursue insulation as their policy preferences diverge from those of the president.

Members of Congress care not only about the preferences of the president today but also about the likely preferences of the president in the future. Members of the majority party in divided government, for example, look to the next election hopefully, wishing for a new president of their party. However, they are realists. If they expect the current party to maintain the White House, they will have a greater incentive to insulate. On the other hand, if the majority and the president are from the same party, majority members hope their party will control the White House after the next election. If they are likely to succeed, they are less likely to insulate.

Proposition 2: Members of Congress assess presidential preferences at the point of decision and likely presidential preferences in the future when deciding about insulating an agency.

Whether or not legislators successfully insulate a new agency depends not only upon their *incentives* but also upon their *ability*. Passing legislation in Congress is difficult. Congress is designed in large part to enhance the reelection prospects of individual members rather than to facilitate collective action (Mayhew 1974). Individual members, determined minorities, and the president frequently stymie the passage of legislation favored by a majority of the members (see, e.g., Brady and Volden 1998; Krehbiel 1998). As a consequence, the majority often must choose between no agency and an agency that at least partially reflects the interests of the president and the minority in Congress.

At each step in the legislative process individual members of Congress can halt a piece of legislation. Committee chairs can refuse to hold hearings on a bill, the Rules Committee can prevent legislation from coming to the floor for a vote, or the Speaker can refuse to schedule a vote. Individual senators can filibuster legislation. Only a cloture vote of sixty senators can overcome a filibuster. Senators can also place anonymous holds on pieces of legislation. Finally, all legislation is subject to a presidential veto. To override a veto, Congress must muster two-thirds majorities in both chambers, something very difficult to do considering presidential partisans usually far exceed the necessary one-third to stop an override attempt. The process of building a coalition to ensure passage of legislation is time-consuming, difficult, and fraught with obstacles. Individual members retain substantial authority to delay legislation through the use of dilatory procedural motions.

The obvious implication is that members of Congress who want to remove new agencies from presidential control must be numerous enough and cohesive enough to overcome these legislative barriers. Scholars disagree about how best to describe the aggregation process or measure the capability of Congress to overcome its collective action problems. One way is to focus on the size of the majority (and thus the minority) party. Large majorities generally have a higher capacity to coalesce and produce a bill that will be enacted. One difficulty with this approach is that it is harder to capture bipartisan activity or the ease of cross-party agreements. Another way of examining congressional decision making is to look at the cohesiveness of member and chamber preferences to determine the ease of collective action in Congress. When preferences diverge within the chambers or when the chambers disagree, it is hard for Congress to come to agreement. This approach, however, does not account for the collective goods that parties provide and the influence parties can have on votes through agenda control, committee composition, and campaign support.

Whichever way we look at it, the ease with which Congress acts is crucial to presidents' success or failure in getting the types of agency designs they prefer. Presidents have an advantage in legislative action when Congress has collective action problems. Congress is more likely to have to compromise with presidents to pass legislation. In addition, as we will see in Chapter 3, presidents also have a greater ability to act unilaterally when Congress is divided and unable to respond.

> *Proposition 3*: The more difficult it is for Congress to come to agreement, the more likely it is for presidents to get agency designs they prefer.

APPLYING THESE PROPOSITIONS TO A WORLD OF PARTIES

To illustrate and test the above propositions, I will focus on Congress's ability to come to agreement in terms of party size.[1] Put simply, large majorities are better able to accomplish their legislative goals than small majorities are. Small majorities are more susceptible to defections, filibusters, veto threats, and presidential attempts to buy off voters on the margins. As such, we should expect large majorities to get what they want. They are more likely to want insulated agencies during periods of divided government and uninsulated agencies during periods of unified government. This implies that the larger the majority in divided government, the higher the probability that a new agency is insulated. In unified government, however, a larger majority should lower the probability that a new agency is insulated.

What are our expectations, however, when the majority is small? In such circumstances the preferences of the minority will play a larger role in the design of the agency because the majority must compromise in order to pass any legislation at all. Our assumptions about the minority should follow the same logic as the majority. Members of the minority are forward-looking, just as the majority is. They understand the impact that the design of a new agency will have on agency policy. Like the majority, their preferences will be different in unified and divided government. They anticipate the influence of presidents on agency policy through their power to make appointments, propose budgets, and direct administrative actions.

In unified government the minority coalition fears effective presidential control of a new agency. Minority members fear the president's likely influence and consequently prefer to remove the administration from presidential control if they can. Minorities in unified government prefer to insulate new agencies as a means of limiting presidential influence, decreasing effectiveness, and possibly gaining influence over the agency by specifying the type of personnel to head the new agency (see, e.g., Moe 1989). Given a choice between a new administration located in a cabinet department or an independent bipartisan commission, for example, the minority in unified government will prefer the latter, since it makes the administration of policies less explicitly partisan. Presidents serving in unified government are more likely to get the types of structures they prefer when their majority is large.

The Republican minority in 1946 was faced with just such a choice. After World War II, Congress recognized that it had to deal with the proliferation of new administrative agencies created since the Depression. Legislators had to choose how to administer farm credit programs. One proposal supported by the secretary of agriculture would have placed the agency responsible for farm credit programs in the Department of Agriculture. The two other proposals were to place the farm credit programs in a resuscitated Farmers Home Corporation or a new independent Agricultural Credit Agency to be controlled by a bipartisan board appointed for staggered twelve-year terms. Republicans, supported by the American Bankers Association, the National Grange, and Farm Bureau Federation, supported the latter two proposals, arguing that these insulated structures would ensure that loans would be granted on a strictly nonpolitical basis.

In divided government, however, the president shares the policy preferences of the minority. The minority supports his appointments, his policies for the new agency, and his budget requests. As such, minority members prefer less insulation and more presidential influence. Since the minority is less likely to agree to insulate in divided government, we should expect that, ceteris paribus, agencies created by small majorities in unified government are more likely to be insulated than agencies created by small majorities in divided government. Presidents facing an opposition Congress will be more influential the smaller the majority.

The position of the Republican minority in the Johnson and Reagan administrations toward the proper type of administration for the nation's maritime policies is a good example of how unified and divided government can change the perspective of the minority in Congress. In 1966, President Johnson proposed consolidating control of the nation's transportation programs into a new Department of Transportation. Part of Johnson's proposal removed the Maritime Administration from the Department of Commerce and placed it squarely within the new Department of Transportation (Johnson 1966, 1:250). The House Republican Policy Committee objected, arguing that the transfer could "perpetuate the present trouble-ridden mismanagement of the maritime crisis" (*Congressional Quarterly Almanac* 1966, 783). They supported instead the creation of an independent maritime agency. The House subsequently passed an amendment to the Department of Transportation bill (261–117) to exclude maritime activities. Johnson lamented that maritime activities were excluded from the bill in his signing statement and ultimately pocket vetoed a bill creating an independent maritime administration (Johnson 1966, 1188; *Congress and the Nation: 1965– 1968*, 243). Thus the Maritime Administration continued in the Department of Commerce. In 1981, the next time Republicans had a chance to express their opinion, Congress passed by voice vote a measure transferring the Maritime Administration to the Department of Transportation, where President Johnson and the House Democratic Party Leadership had proposed to place it all along. The Republican minority's

Size of Majority

	Small	Large
Unified Government	Higher	Lower
Divided Government	Lower	Higher

FIGURE 1.1   Impact of Majority Size on the Probability of Insulation

change of heart came with the accession of Ronald Reagan to the presidency. They no longer favored an independent maritime agency because
they shared the policy preferences of Reagan and his likely political appointees to the Department of Transportation.

Figure 1.1 summarizes our expectations about insulation in terms of parties and unified and divided government. Our expectation is that during
periods of divided government the probability that a new agency will be insulated is higher, provided the majority is large enough. The majority wor-
ries about the president's influence on the new agency and attempts to
shield it. When the majority in divided government is small, they cannot
overcome presidential opposition to insulation.

Our prediction in unified government is that the probability of insulation is low, provided again that the majority is large enough. When the majority in unified government is small, however, it must compromise with a
minority that wants insulation in order to protect it from effective presidential control of a new agency.[2] So although presidents benefit when Congress cannot come to agreement, this is a case where Congress can come to
agreement but the agreement is inconsistent with presidential preferences.
Members of the majority, based upon their institutional position, are more
concerned with passing legislation than protecting the president's influence. If the choice is between an insulated agency and no agency at all, the
small majority will choose the insulated agency.

If we assume for a moment that majority size is constant, we can make
predictions about the impact of presidential durability as well. In Figure 1.2
I do just this. In divided government, agencies are more likely to be insulated if the president appears durable. Members of the majority worry

Presidential Durability

	Low	High
Unified Government	Higher	Lower
Divided Government	Lower	Higher

FIGURE 1.2 Impact of Presidential Durability on the Probability of Insulation

about the president's continuing influence on the agency. If the president is vulnerable, however, they will forestall insulation in anticipation of a president who shares their preferences. In unified government, the majority prefers more presidential control so long as the president or someone like him likely will be in office for a while. If the president is weak, the majority is more likely to insulate in anticipation of a new opposition president.

Of course, like the majority, the minority evaluates the durability of the president and takes this into account when making decisions about insulation. Even during periods of divided government, a minority may support insulation if there exists strong evidence that the president will not be reelected. Similarly, during periods of unified government members of the minority may actually be more likely to support an uninsulated agency if they anticipate the election of a president from their party. I will deal with this in more detail in Chapter 5.

These predictions present neat, all-else-equal predictions about the politics of agency design based in a theory of congressional and presidential incentives and power. We can test these predictions with quantitative data on agencies created in the United States, and it is to this task that I turn in the next chapter.

AGENCY DESIGN, SEPARATION OF POWERS, AND POLICY PREFERENCES

Harry Truman had the unique experience of serving in both branches of government. When he was in Congress he supported the creation of administrative agencies that were insulated from presidential control. The product of the actions of Truman and his colleagues in Congress was a transportation policy that was fragmented, uncoordinated, and unresponsive to the presidential direction that could have remedied these problems. Truman's experience illustrates how the separation of powers sets up a struggle over agency design based upon the unique perspective of each branch. Placing new authority over maritime, aeronautical, and railroad policy in distinct independent commissions made sense to Truman as a member of Congress. It gave to each policy a priority and independence, and each agency's commission structure ensured that decisions would be made independent of presidential considerations.

In isolation, each decision was reasonable, but in the aggregate President Truman was left with transportation policy decided by appointees, some of whom came from past administrations. These appointees made decisions with only their part of transportation policy in mind, leaving transportation policy for which Truman was responsible needlessly fragmented and unresponsive.

Truman's case illustrates how the separation of powers creates disagreements over agency design. Each branch has a different perspective on the design of administrative agencies and the administrative state based upon its position in our constitutional system. Modern presidents take a larger view based upon their position as chief executive and their national election constituency. Members of Congress make decisions about agency design on more proximate concerns tied to reelection interests, not an aggregate picture of administrative rationality. The bureaucracy reflects the agreements, disagreements, and negotiations of the branches over time subject to the constraints of the courts and the Constitution.

Although the perspectives and powers of each branch are shaped by our constitutional system, the separation of powers is not the whole story. The ratifiers of the Constitution did not anticipate the demise of deliberation and the immediate rise of political parties. Since Congress and the president would share in the responsibility of designing the administrative state, so partisan politics would play a role in agency design. When legislators share the president's policy preferences, they help create agencies with substantial executive influence. Their hope is that presidents will appoint like-minded agency heads, provide necessary direction through executive directives, and propose adequate funding levels in future budgets, thereby ensuring a more effective implementation of the policy these members prefer.

Even in cases where substantial opposition to the president exists in Congress, presidents can prevail. Congress's ability to remove agencies from presidential control depends upon the legislators' ability to come to agreement. When Congress lacks the capacity to overcome presidential opposition, presidents are more likely to get the types of agencies they prefer.

Although understanding how preferences shaped by constitutionally dictated institutions provides us leverage on the agency design decision, it does not tell us all that we need to know about the president's role in agency design. We need to look more fully at the president's perspective on agency design and the unique institutional powers presidents have in agency design both in the legislature and through administrative actions like executive orders, departmental orders, and reorganization plans.

Moving from Insulation in Theory to Insulation in Reality

> Presidency research is one of the last bastions of historical, non-quantitative research in American politics.
>
> —Gary King, "Methodology and the Presidency."

One of the primary themes of this book is that agency design is political. This does not mean, however, that agency design is incomprehensible or that there are not predictable regularities over time. On the contrary, the theory presented in the last chapter produced a number of propositions about the politics of agency design depending upon preference divergence, presidential durability, and Congress's ability to come to agreement. These propositions were operationalized into a series of predictions about the probability that new agencies would be insulated depending upon divided government, presidential durability, and majority size. In particular, the predictions highlight cases where presidents should get the types of agencies they prefer, such as when a significant number of members of Congress share the president's preferences or when Congress cannot come to agreement.

Thus far, the discussion of the theory has only included individual case examples used for illustrative purposes. Although helpful, these do not prove that the theory is consistent with the reality of how U.S. government agencies are created. To provide more confidence in the general applicability of the theory, I collected data on all U.S. government agencies created by legislation between 1946 and 1997.[1] I use this data to test whether factors like policy disagreements between Congress and the president, congressional calculations about presidential durability, and congressional capacity to overcome collective action problems alter the probability that a new agency will be insulated from political control.

These new data provide a unique opportunity to test what has heretofore been untested.[2] They allow me to analyze agency design directly, rather than indirectly through the congressional delegation decision. They also allow for the proper controls and, later, direct tests of the president's influence in the agency design process.

THE DATA

I gathered data on all administrative agencies created in the United States between 1946 and 1997, excluding advisory commissions, multilateral agencies, and educational and research institutions. The list was compiled using the *United States Government Manual* (*USGM*). Each agency created during this period is one observation in the data set, and each is coded according to structural characteristics indicating insulation from presidential control at the time of its creation.[3] An analysis of the design of administrative agencies at the time they were created is important, for as Harold Seidman (1998, 138) argues, "The first organization decision is crucial. The course of institutional development may be set irrevocably by the initial choice of administrative agency and by the how the program is designed."

What Is Considered a New Agency?

Defining what organizations are agencies is straightforward. Section 512 of the Administrative Procedures Act states:

> "Agency" means each authority of the Government . . . whether or not it
> is within or subject to review by another agency, but does not include—
> (A) the Congress, (B) the courts of the United States, (C) the government
> of the territories or possessions of the United States, (D) the government
> of the District of Columbia.

In essence, an agency is anything that is not Congress, a court in the judicial branch, or the D.C. or territorial governments. The determination of what constitutes a *new* agency is not a trivial consideration (see, e.g., Emmerich 1971; Whitnah 1983). Political actors create and terminate agencies frequently, but they rarely terminate the functions these bureaucracies perform (Daniels 1997). New organizational units often perform functions similar to those of previously existing agencies. In this data set an agency was considered to be new if it had a new name and different functions from any previously existing agencies. So, for example, the National Archives and Records Service (NARS), created in the General Services Administration in 1949, is considered a new agency even though it retained much of the character of the National Archives Establishment, a previously existing independent agency. In addition to a change in location, the NARS had a new name and was given new responsibilities over federal government records. On the other hand, the data set excludes the Social Security Administration (SSA), which became an independent agency in 1995. Although the newly independent SSA adopted some new responsibilities when it became independent, its name did not change.

Bureaucracies vary in size from cabinet departments, major administrations, and bureaus to offices and programs. The data set includes cabinet departments, administrations, bureaus, and large offices. It excludes programs and offices not large enough to be included in the *USGM*. So, for example, the data set includes the Office of Economic Opportunity, a significant part of President Johnson's War on Poverty, but excludes the Learn and Serve America program run through the Corporation for National and Community Service. The data set is subject to the criticism that it includes too many trivial organizational units. Inclusion or exclusion from the *USGM*, however, provides an easy, unbiased decision rule. All previous attempts to list new agencies created since World War II depend upon the subjective assessment of individual scholars (Emmerich 1971; Whitnah 1983). Inclusion in the *USGM* also indicates a level of importance. In addition, quantitative analysis can include controls for the relative importance of new agencies, parsing out the effects of size or importance on the degree of insulation. Consequently, it is better to include too many rather than too few.

It is important to realize that administrative agencies are rarely created new out of whole cloth, regardless of size, function, or origination. New agencies invariably combine existing personnel, resources, appropriations, and delegated functions into a new administrative unit. This administrative unit is usually delegated new authority and appropriated new funds to carry out the mission it was designed to perform. Most authorizing legislation includes separate sections dealing with the transfer of personnel and appropriations. As such, the definition of what constitutes a new agency can play an important role in the study of agency creation.

Why the 1946–97 Period?

The 1946–97 period provides a number of advantages for testing the theories of agency design. First, by 1946 the forms of government administration were largely settled (Horn 1995). The advantages and drawbacks of different types of administrative structures for different parties were well known (Bernstein 1977; Cushman 1972; Peterson 1985). Legal questions over the president's appointment and removal powers were largely settled. Second, the post-1946 era is a period of relative stability in congressional oversight of the bureaucracy. The Administrative Procedures Act (APA) and the Legislative Reorganization Act, which were enacted in 1946, fundamentally changed congressional oversight of the bureaucracy. The APA established procedures governing rule making by administrative agencies. The act, among other things, required notification of and participation by the relevant interests subject to the new rules. The inclusion of the relevant interests in agency decisions ensured that interested parties would notify congressional committees of any controversial agency actions (McCubbins and Schwartz 1984). The Legislative Reorganization Act, in addition to stabilizing the committee system, mandated that all House and Senate committees apply "continuous watchfulness" to agencies under their jurisdiction.[4] Finally, 1946 is also widely acknowledged as the time of transition to the modern presidency. Franklin Roosevelt created modern expectations of strong presidential leadership in both legislation and management (Lewis and Strine 1996; Neustadt 1960). President Truman was the first modern president fully encumbered with the expectation of legislative leadership and top-down administrative management. As such, 1946–97 is a period of relative stability in administrative action, legislative oversight, and presidential goals and expectations.

How Many New Agencies Were Created?

The administrative state grew tremendously during the 1946–97 period in the United States. The expansion of the bureaucracy began in the 1930s owing to the New Deal and the World War II mobilization effort. Once in

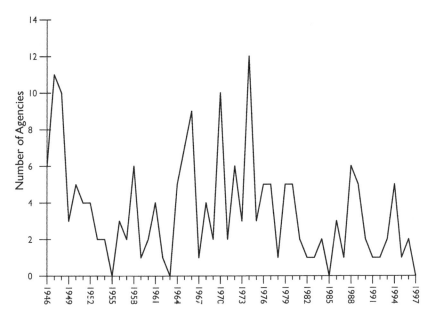

FIGURE 2.1   Number of Agencies Created by Legislation

place, the burgeoning administrative structures of the New Deal and war effort were not easily dismantled. Figure 2.1 shows the number of administrative agencies created by legislation during this period. In total, Congress created 182 agencies.

There is substantial variation in the number of new agencies year to year. The greatest administrative growth took place during the Truman administration and the administrations of President Johnson and President Nixon. The single most productive Congress was the 80th Congress (1947–48), which created twenty-one agencies, including the National Military Establishment, the Economic Cooperation Administration, and the Federal Mediation and Conciliation Service. In the years immediately following the World War II era, Congress and the president were left with the difficult task of reshaping the administrative structures that were rather haphazardly created during the Depression and the war. This involved the dissolution, reorganization, and creation of a number of administrative agencies. President Johnson's Great Society Program also increased the size of the bureaucracy, with sixteen new agencies created by the 89th Congress (1965–66). A surprising amount of growth also occurred during the Nixon administration. Twelve agencies were created between 1969 and 1970, and fifteen between 1973 and 1974. Among the more prominent are the National Highway Traffic Safety Administration, Amtrak, and the Consumer Product Safety Commission.

What Types of Insulation? The Dependent Variable

The bureaucracy can loosely be divided into administrative agencies inside the cabinet and those placed outside of it. Since the executive power is vested in the president by Article 2 of the U.S. Constitution, the first administrative agencies were created as cabinet departments under presidential control. Today, most of the administrative apparatus of the United States is part of this cabinet structure and ostensibly under presidential direction. This is reinforced by the president's ability to nominate and remove appointees at the top levels of the cabinet. The remainder of executive functions are dispersed throughout the other branches or placed outside the cabinet in independent establishments or government corporations.

Some executive-type functions, for example, are lodged in the legislative or judicial branch. The Government Printing Office is located in the legislative branch, as is the Botanic Garden. Most administrative activities in the legislative branch, however, have some nominal relation to congressional activity. The Architect of the Capitol, for example, operates and maintains the capitol buildings and grounds. The Congressional Budget Office provides Congress with basic budget data and analyses. Other executive-type agencies like the U.S. Sentencing Commission and the Federal Judicial Center reside in the judicial branch. Although these agencies, again, seem naturally located within the judicial branch, their location is not necessarily assured by their function.[5]

The rest have been placed outside the executive branch in independent agencies or government corporations. Agencies like the National Aeronautics and Space Administration and the Environmental Protection Agency are examples. So, too, are the independent regulatory commissions like the Federal Trade Commission, Federal Communications Commission, and Consumer Product Safety Commission, or government corporations like the Reconstruction Finance Corporation or Amtrak.

Politicians who insulate want to decrease presidential influence and the impact of changing administrations on agency policies. There are a number

FIGURE 2.2   Agency Location Measure

of ways that agencies can be insulated from presidential control. Location is one means of insulation, particularly insulation from political control (Epstein and O'Halloran 1999; Khademian 1996; Seidman 1998; Wood and Waterman 1994). Congress purposefully chooses to place new agencies outside of the Executive Office of the President (EOP) or cabinet as a way of shielding the agencies from presidential influence. The president exercises less influence over independent commissions, government corporations, and agencies in the legislative or judicial branches (Emmerich 1971; Seidman 1981, 1998).

All agencies in the data set have been coded with a number between 1 and 5 according to their location in the federal government (see Figure 2.2).[6] Agencies in the EOP (10 percent) are coded with a 1, the cabinet (46 percent) a 2, independent agencies (13 percent) a 3, independent commissions (19 percent) a 4, and government corporations or other (12 percent) a 5. This implicitly assumes that administrative agencies can be ordered according to their insulation from presidential control. The assumption is that agencies in the EOP are the least insulated, followed by cabinet agencies. Next are independent agencies like the National Aeronautics and Space Administration (NASA) and the Small Business Administration (SBA). Independent commissions like the Securities and Exchange Commission (SEC) and the Equal Employment Opportunity Commission (EEOC) follow. The final category includes government corporations like Amtrak and the Virgin Islands Corporation and agencies outside the executive branch like the General Accounting Office (legislative branch) and the U.S. Sentencing Commission (judicial branch).

However, location outside the cabinet or the EOP is arguably an indicator rather than a cause of diminished presidential influence. What makes agencies outside the cabinet less amenable to presidential control? Agencies outside the EOP or cabinet usually have one or more of the characteristics of independent regulatory commissions.

The first of these characteristics is *independence*, meaning that a new agency is created with no layers of bureaucratic organization above it. Independent agencies are immune to the pressures and larger policy goals of executive departments that threaten administrative agencies. The budget process for each fiscal year begins with agencies and programs submitting their budget requests to agency heads. The secretaries or directors then respond to the proposed request in light of the needs of the whole department or agency. Agencies placed outside of existing structures are removed from these budget pressures and can lobby the Office of Management and Budget (OMB) and the White House directly for their position, something subsidiary agencies are less able to do. Supporters of the Social Security Administration (SSA), for example, worked since the early 1970s to remove it from the Department of Health, Education, and Welfare (HEW, HHS) and make it independent. They lamented budgetary pressures and departmental regulations that did not take into account the special needs of the SSA. They achieved their goal in 1994 when the SSA became an independent agency (*Congressional Quarterly Almanac* 1994, 662–63).

Each agency that is created with no layers of bureaucratic organization above it is coded with a 1, and all other agencies are coded with a 0. In total, 37 percent, or sixty-seven, of the agencies created since 1946 are independent. An agency that is coded as independent is not necessarily the same as an "independent agency" created outside the cabinet. For example, the Department of Education, created in 1977, is independent since it has no layers of bureaucratic organization above it. On the other hand, the Foreign Service Labor Relations Board, created in 1980, is located outside the cabinet but is not independent since it is part of the independent Federal Labor Relations Authority.

Agencies outside the cabinet are also frequently boards or *commissions*. Governance by a board or commission insulates new agencies from presidential control by increasing the number of actors who must be influenced to change the direction of an agency. The creation of the Federal Reserve is a good example. Bankers explicitly favored governance of the Federal Reserve by a board rather than a single appointed official because they believed that it would be easier to protect a board from political influence than a single individual. They also believed that a board would provide greater opportunity for the representation of banking interests in governance (Cushman 1972). In total, eighty, or 44 percent, of the agencies created by legislation since 1946 are governed by boards or commissions. Among them are the National Security Council, the Equal Employment Opportunity Commission, and the Corporation for National Community Service.

The administrators of agencies outside the immediate control of the president also frequently serve for *fixed terms*. Political appointees who serve for fixed terms are insulated from presidential control since they cannot be removed without cause. In fact many such appointees carry over from previous administrations. They are granted more independence than those political appointees who serve at the pleasure of the president. The most extreme example of independence from presidential control, of course, is federal judges who serve life terms. In 1988 and 1989 the Democratic majority in Congress attempted to remove the National Park Service from political control. Democrats were angered by what they perceived as "destructive interference" from Republican political appointees in the Department of the Interior during the Reagan administration. In response, the House passed HR 1484, which would have granted the Park Service director a five-year term and independence from the secretary of interior in all day-to-day functions of the Park Service.[7] Fifty-six, or 31 percent, of the agencies created since 1946 have political appointees that serve for fixed terms. Among the most recognizable are the Atomic Energy Commission, the National Science Foundation, and the Federal Election Commission.

Finally, *specific qualifications for administrators* are a means of insulation. In most agencies, the president can nominate any person of his choice to lead the new agency. Sometimes, however, specific limitations based upon political party, occupation, or experience are attached to new appointments. These are a means of limiting presidential discretion. Seidman (1998, 19) argues, for example, that congressional attempts to specify participants on the National Security Council "properly could be construed as a ploy by the Republican Congress to circumscribe the Democratic president's powers in areas in which he was constitutionally supreme." The most extreme limitation on presidential appointment is party-balancing limitations on government commissions. Statutes creating most of the independent regulatory commissions, for example, require that "no more than *x* members of the commission can be from one political party." These limitations are an attempt to keep partisanship out of administration. Seventy-four, or 41 percent, of the agencies created by legislation since 1946 have specific qualifications for administrators. Twenty-one of these seventy-four have party-balancing limitations.

Of the 182 agencies created by legislation between 1946 and 1997, 64 percent have at least one of the insulating characteristics described above. Twenty-nine, or 16 percent, have all four insulating characteristics. Of course, not all agencies are insulated in the same manner. The National Transportation Safety Board, for example, is a five-member commission with fixed terms and party-balancing limitations on appointments, but it was initially located squarely within a cabinet department, the Department of Transportation.

These forms of insulation from presidential control clearly diminish the ability of presidents to set administration policy and control the day-to-day workings of administrative agencies. They also insulate these agencies from congressional control, although not to the degree that they insulate the agencies from presidential control. Agencies that are made independent have been extracted from the larger budget battles of the cabinet departments and are better able to lobby the OMB and Congress directly for their budgets. Indeed, supporters of an independent Maritime Administration claimed that the placement of the Maritime Administration in the Department of Commerce in the 1950s had led to its neglect in Congress and the administration (*Congressional Quarterly Almanac* 1966, 784). One of the primary reasons interest groups push for independent agencies is that greater prestige is often attached to independent agencies during the budget process in both the administration and Congress.

Agencies that are governed by boards or commissions are as immune to direction from Congress as from the president. The number of appointees who must be influenced to change policy is increased for the president and Congress equally. Finally, agencies headed by appointees who serve for fixed terms and whose qualifications have been specified by executive decree or statute are by design immune from nonstatutory controls exercised by congressional committees in Congress of one type or another.[8] The Federal Election Commission (FEC), for example, is composed of six members, three Democrats and three Republicans, who serve for fixed terms. In order for the Republican majority in Congress to exert influence over the FEC, it must convince not only the three Republican members to alter agency policy, but also a Democratic member.

THE CAUSES OF INSULATION

Having identified different indicators of insulation in the design of administrative agencies, we can now determine the impact of divided government, presidential durability, and majority strength on the probability that a new agency will be insulated. The percentage of new agencies designed with insulating characteristics varies substantially over time. Several patterns emerge, however. First, there is a higher percentage of agencies with insulating characteristics during periods of divided government, particularly when the majority is strong. Second, presidential durability appears to correlate with the percentage of new agencies that have insulating characteristics. On the one hand, during periods of unified government presidents who appear durable are correlated with fewer insulated agencies being created. On the other hand, during periods of divided government, the durability of the president is correlated with a larger number of agencies being insulated.

Figure 2.3 includes graphs of the number of new agencies created during 1946–97 with the different insulating characteristics. For reference each graph includes the total number of agencies created by legislation during the same period. Even in the raw numbers several patterns emerge from the graphs. There is some clustering of the number of agencies created with insulating characteristics. Relatively few insulated agencies were created during the Kennedy, Johnson, and Carter administrations. A larger number were created during the Nixon and Ford administrations.

Of course, an examination of the counts masks an increase in the number of insulated agencies owing to an overall increase in the number of agencies created during that year. Figure 2.4 includes graphs of the percentage of new agencies created during 1946–97 with different insulating characteristics. I calculated percentages by Congress, or two-year periods, since there were a few years during which no agencies were created. Some care is therefore necessary in interpreting the percentages, since the presence or

FIGURE 2.3 Number of Legislatively Created Agencies with Different
Characteristics of Insulation, 1946–97

Agencies Placed Outside Cabinet

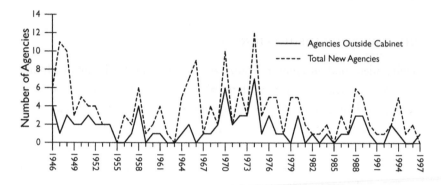

Number of Commissions

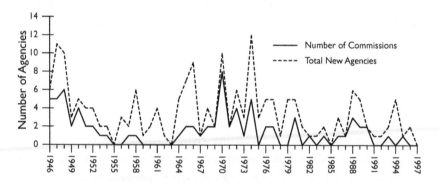

Agencies with Specific Qualifications for Political Appointees

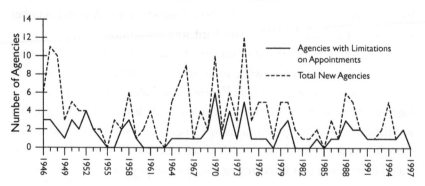

Number of Independent Agencies

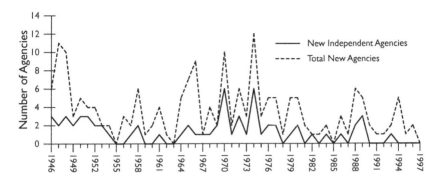

Agencies with Fixed Terms

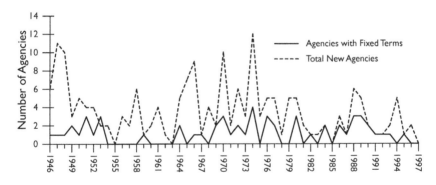

FIGURE 2.4 Percentage of New Agencies Created by Legislation with
Insulating Characteristics, 1946–97

Percentage Outside Cabinet

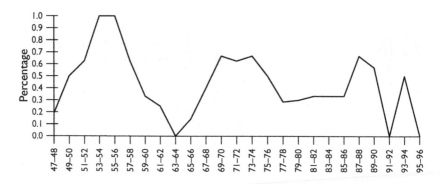

Percentage of New Agencies that are Commissions

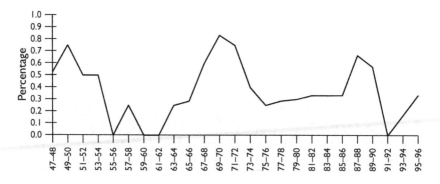

Percentage with Specific Qualifications for Appointees

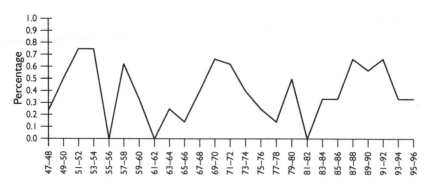

Percentage Independent

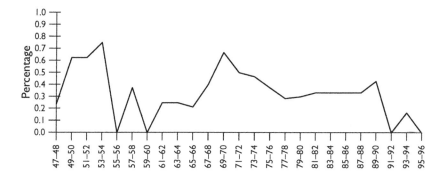

Percentage with Fixed Terms

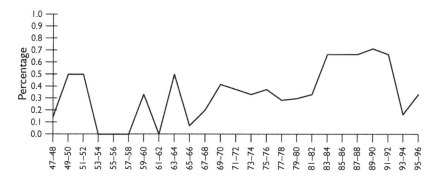

absence of one insulating agency can result in a large change in probability if few agencies were created during a two-year period. In particular, only a few agencies were created in parts of the Eisenhower (1955–56, three agencies; 1959–60, three agencies), Reagan (1981–86, nine agencies), Bush (1991–92, two agencies), and Clinton administrations (1995–97, three agencies).

Even with these limitations, several patterns emerge from Figure 2.4. The percentage of new agencies with insulating characteristics correlates with periods of divided government. The periods with the highest percentage of insulated agencies are the Nixon and Ford administrations, both periods of divided government. Similarly, the periods with the lowest percentages of insulation are the Kennedy, Johnson, and Carter administrations, all periods of unified government. Indeed, the Reagan and Bush administrations, while having few total agencies created, also appear to have a relatively high percentage of new agencies insulated from political control. It is also interesting to note that periods of divided government with large majorities have higher percentages of insulated agencies than do periods of divided government with smaller majorities. Large majorities are better able to insulate in divided government than small majorities.

The correlation of presidential durability with the percentage of insulated agencies is less clear. When presidents are weak during periods of unified government, the percentage of insulated new agencies appears to increase. The Democratic majority did insulate more during 1951–52 when Truman's public approval had dropped into the twenties. Similarly, the Democratic majority appears to seek insulation more late in Johnson's administration. Johnson's average public approval of 66 percent in 1965 had dropped to 41 percent by 1968, and the percentage of new insulated agencies also appears to increase. During periods of divided government, however, a weak president seems correlated with a lower percentage of insulated agencies. Late in the Nixon administration and during the Ford administration the percentage of new insulated agencies decreases.

To each of these generalizations there are exceptions. For example, during the 1947–48 period there appears to be no pattern. It is a period of divided government with a weak president, and the percentage of new insulated agencies is generally low except that there were a relatively high percentage of commissions created during the period. During the Carter administration, the percentage of insulated agencies does not increase, even though Carter's approval ratings are low. Still, the graph suggests that electoral uncertainty, divided government, and presidential durability all appear to have some relationship with insulation. The estimation of econometric models in the next two sections will allow us to parse out the effects of each factor on the probability that a new agency is insulated.

One difficulty with examining the 1946–97 period is that most years of unified government are years when Democrats control the Congress and White House. Conversely, most years of divided government have a Republican in the White House. Another explanation for the patterns would be that Democrats prefer less insulation than Republicans do. This is not plausible, however, since there is no reason to believe that Republicans want any less political interference in agency decision making than Democrats do. Indeed, it was the Republican Congress of 1947–48 that created the Hoover Commission to reorganize the executive branch with an eye toward presidential control. Both types of agencies have been created under each administration.

Econometric Models: Variables and Methods

Graphs of the number of agencies created with such characteristics provide some evidence for bivariate relationships between the factors and insulation. The estimation of econometric models, however, provides a means of testing for a statistically significant relationship between each causal factor and the probability that a new agency is insulated while controlling for other factors such as agency size. The econometric models also estimate the magnitude of each factor on the probability of insulation.

Variables

Both the theory and Figures 2.3 and 2.4 suggest that more insulation occurs in periods of divided government. Since majorities are more likely to want to insulate during periods of divided government, I include an indicator variable for divided government that is coded 1 if the president and the majorities in the House and Senate do not all share the same party affiliation and 0 otherwise. Of the 182 agencies created by legislation, 106, or 59 percent, were created during a period of divided government.

Of course, the ability of the majority to insulate a new agency in divided government depends upon the strength of the majority. As such, all specifications include an interaction term. I interact measures of majority strength with divided government. The interaction terms should be positive, indicating that measures of majority strength increase the probability that a new agency will be insulated during periods of divided government.

To measure Congress's ability to come to agreement or congressional strength, I use the size of the majority in the House of Representatives at the time an agency is created. The mean value is 59 percent, and it varies from a low of 50 percent to 68 percent. In other specifications I have included size of the majority in the House of Representatives, size of the majority in the Senate, or the smaller of the two with similar results.

A second measure of congressional strength is the length of time the majority has been in power. I measure this length of time by counting the number of elections since the majority was last out of power in either the House or the Senate. So agencies created in 1947–48 are coded with a 0, since the party became the majority in the aftermath of the 1946 election. Agencies created in 1981–82 are also coded with a 0, since the Republicans gained control of the Senate in the 1980 election. The mean value is four elections. For both measures of congressional strength the coefficient should be negative, indicating that an increase in strength (larger majority, longer time in the majority) causes a lower probability of a new agency being insulated in unified government.

The durability of the president also plays an important role in the calculation of the majority. I measure the likelihood of the president's reelection using the president's approval rating at the time the new agency is created.[9] Since 1938 the Gallup Opinion Poll has asked some variant of the question "Do you approve or disapprove of the way President _____ is handling his job as president?" This provides a good, unbiased assessment of the reelection prospects of the president's party at the time of agency creation. The value varies from a low of 24 percent to 79 percent and has a mean of 51 percent.

Since the reelection prospects of the president should have a different impact in unified and divided government, I interact approval rating with divided government. The coefficient on the term should be positive, since a high approval rating (and higher reelection chances) should increase the probability that a new agency is insulated during periods of divided government. The coefficient on approval rating itself (principal effect) should be negative, since high approval should decrease the probability that a new agency will be insulated during periods of unified government. Since the president can be elected to only two terms, I implicitly assume with the use of approval ratings that high approval ratings in the president's second term also signal the likely election of a successor from the president's party.[10]

The impact of presidential durability is mediated through the majority's ability to get what it wants. As suggested in Chapter 1, for example, a weak majority in unified government may want to insulate more if the president is also weak, but it may not be able to get what it wants. Majority members will have to compromise with the minority. I assume that approval rating has the same impact on the probability of insulation when the majority is large and when the majority is small. Holding majority size constant, increasing presidential durability should lead to a lower probability of insulation in unified government and a higher probability of insulation in divided government. This is something I will deal with in greater detail in Chapter 5.

Controls

Finally, I include controls for the importance of the agency and the possibility of a trend. Importance is measured by an indicator variable for whether or not an agency has a line in the budget. Most large agencies have their own line in the budget, and such a designation represents a level of budget review by OMB and congressional appropriators that smaller agencies do not have. Seventy-one percent of the agencies have their own line in the budget. I have also estimated models using the log of each agency's initial budget in 1992 dollars or an indicator variable for agencies mentioned *Congress and the Nation* in the year they were created as measures of agency importance.[11] These models confirm what is reported in the main text. I also include a trend term to eliminate false correlations owing to similar trends over time. The trend measure is coded 1 for agencies created in 1946, 2 for agencies created in 1947, and so on.

Methods

I have identified five different indicators of insulation: agency location, independence, governance by board or commission, fixed terms for political appointees, and mandated qualifications for political appointees. I estimate two econometric models of each insulating characteristic. The first specification for each includes majority size as the measure of congressional strength, and the second includes length of time in the majority. I estimate ordered probit models for the agency location measure since it is a discrete, ordered variable.[12] Bivariate probit models are estimated for the other indicators of insulation.[13]

RESULTS AND DISCUSSION

Table 2.1 presents the estimates of the models of agency insulation.[14] The results confirm my expectations about the impact of divided government, presidential durability, and majority strength on the probability of insulation. Each model improves significantly on the null model, and the independent variables measuring divided government, presidential durability, and majority strength generally perform according to expectations. Congress is more likely to insulate during periods of divided government when the majority is strong. Legislators also appear sensitive to the durability of the president when deciding whether or not to insulate.

One of the advantages of both ordered probit models and bivariate probit models is that coefficients can be interpreted according to their impact on the probability that an agency will fall into one of the ordered categories. For example, the agency location measure has five categories according to proximity to presidential control. Simulations run altering the hypothetical values of different independent variables can determine the impact those variables have on the probability that an agency will fall into one of the five categories. If we are interested in determining the impact of presidential approval ratings, for example, we can hold all other independent variables constant and vary presidential approval ratings in simulations to see how they affect the probability that a new agency will be placed in the cabinet or in one of the other categories.[15]

Unified and Divided Government

One of the most interesting outcomes of the econometric models is that the indicator for divided government is significant in most models and is *negative*. On its face, this appears to indicate that agencies are less likely to be insulated during periods of divided government, contrary to expectations. Care is necessary in interpreting these coefficients in isolation from

TABLE 2.1

ML Estimates of Probit Models of Insulation in U.S. Government Agencies, 1946–97

Variable	Location (1)	Location (2)	Independence (3)	Independence (4)	Commission (5)	Commission (6)	Fixed Terms (7)	Fixed Terms (8)	Limitations on Appointments (9)	Limitations on Appointments (10)
Electoral uncertainty										
Majority size	-0.08**	—	-0.06**	—	-0.04**	—	-0.05*	—	-0.11**	—
Length in majority	—	-0.05*	—	-0.04*	—	-0.03	—	-0.08*	—	-0.07**
Divided government (0,1)	-4.33**	-0.78	-4.71**	-1.90**	-2.37	-1.77**	-7.34**	-1.60**	-6.02**	-1.86**
Majority Strength										
Majority size * DG	0.07**	—	0.64**	—	0.02	—	0.11**	—	0.08**	—
Length in majority * DG	—	0.10**	—	0.13**	—	0.08*	—	-0.08*	—	0.11**
Presidential durability										
Approval rating	-0.006	-0.011*	-0.007	-0.012*	-0.014**	-0.017**	-0.022*	-0.027*	-0.010	-0.017*
Approval rating * DG	-0.003	0.006	0.015*	0.025**	0.026**	0.033**	0.026**	0.029*	0.020*	0.030**
Controls and cut points										
Line in the budget (0,1)	0.10	0.07	0.81**	0.79**	0.10	0.09	0.15	0.09	-0.39**	-0.39**
Trend	0.02**	0.01**	0.00	-0.01	-0.01	-0.01*	0.02**	0.02**	0.01	0.00
Constant	—	—	3.41**	0.09	3.07**	0.93**	2.89**	0.42	6.90**	1.05**
Number of cases	180	180	180	180	180	180	180	180	180	180
χ^2 (7 df)	11.96*	18.73**	20.49**	41.68**	16.74**	14.44**	24.95**	15.58**	29.72**	13.30**

NOTE: Cut points omitted from table (−5.94, −4.44, −4.08, −3.37, −1.83, −0.34, 0.01, 0.71). ** Significant at the .05 level, * significant at the .10 level in one-tailed test of significance. Standard errors are estimated using the robust estimator of variance proposed by Huber (1967) and White (1980, 1982) and adjusted for clustering on year. Dependent variable for models 1, 2 is a five-category ordinal variable of agency location—(1) EOP; (2) cabinet; (3) independent agency; (4) independent commission; (5) government corporation or other.

the interaction effects, however. In each model, majority size is significant and negative, indicating that agencies created in unified government under larger majorities have lower probabilities of insulation. The interaction terms are all positive and significant, indicating either that the larger majorities matter less in divided government or that agencies are more likely to be insulated in divided government when the majority is large, consistent with my expectations.

Figure 2.5 graphs the change in the probability that a new agency will have one of the insulating characteristics depending upon the size of the majority. The solid line reflects the impact of majority size in unified government, and the dotted line the impact in divided government. What is clear is that strong majorities in unified government clearly get what they want: uninsulated agencies. In divided government, increasing majority size increases the probability of insulation in two out of five models. Importantly, the probability of insulation is higher in divided government in each case, provided the majority is large enough, at the mean or slightly higher.

These results are corroborated by the results using the length of time the majority has been in power as a measure of congressional strength. The longer a majority has been in power in divided government, the higher the probability a new agency will be insulated. The longer a majority has been in power in unified government, the lower the probability of insulation. Figure 2.6 graphs the change in the probability that a new agency will have one of the insulating characteristics by the length of time the majority is in power. The crisscross pattern shows clearly how stronger majorities are less likely to insulate in unified government and more likely to insulate in divided government.

Majority Strength

My main predictions with regard to congressional strength revolve around the majority's ability to get what it wants. I hypothesized that strong majorities in unified government would want no insulation and that strong majorities in divided government would want insulation. In general, these predictions proved to be true, although less so when I measure Congress's ability to come to agreement or strength with majority size.

What about when the majorities were small? Did they get what they wanted? In each case I hypothesized that majorities would be forced to compromise with the opposition party and that the agency that resulted would be more likely to reflect the minority's interest the smaller the majority got. In unified government, this means majorities get more insulation than they want. It is either an insulated agency or no agency at all. In divided government this means that the majority gets less insulation than it would like. It is either this or no agency at all. Indeed, in cases where the majority was small in unified government and divided government, the results conform to my expectations.

In the end, however, it is difficult to test whether presidents benefit from congressional weakness per se. It is impossible to look at congressional capacity and assess its importance for presidents except in cases where Congress wants to use it. Congress primarily wants to use it to insulate in cases of divided government. And in such cases, presidents clearly do benefit from congressional weakness and the necessity of compromise.[16] One clear way of looking at whether presidents take advantage of congressional weakness, and something I do in Chapter 4, is to look at presidential use of unilateral actions like executive orders to create agencies.

Presidential Durability

When members of Congress make calculations about the need for insulation, they consider the preferences of the president and his likely durability. The estimates indicate that in unified government an increase in presidential durability decreases the probability that a new agency will have one of the insulating characteristics. All of the coefficients are negative, although they are not significant in each specification. On the other hand, the interaction term has a positive coefficient and is significant in most specifications, indicating that during periods of divided government an increase in presidential durability increases the probability that a new agency will have the insulating characteristic.

Majorities that worry about how the president will influence the future direction of an agency are, indeed, more likely to insulate. They worry when the president is weak in unified government and strong in divided government. Figure 2.7 illustrates this with the agency data. The change in probability associated with increasing approval ratings in simulations confirms what the coefficients indicated. In all models except the agency location model an increase in approval rating decreases the probability of insu-

FIGURE 2.5   Impact of Majority Size on the Probability of New Agencies
Having Insulating Characteristics, 1946–97

Location Outside Cabinet

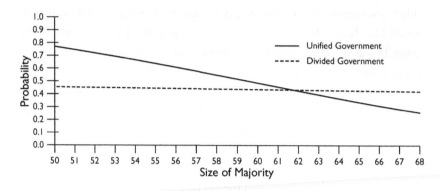

Independence

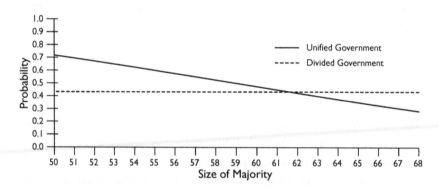

Specific Qualifications for Appointees

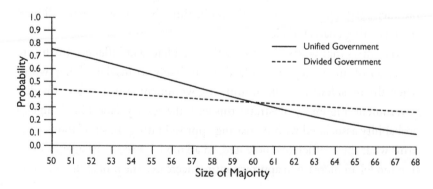

Governance by Commission

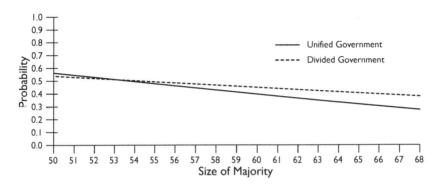

Fixed Terms

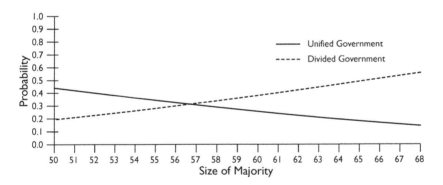

FIGURE 2.6 Impact of Length of Time in Majority on the Probability of New Agencies Having Insulating Characteristics, 1946–97

Location Outside Cabinet

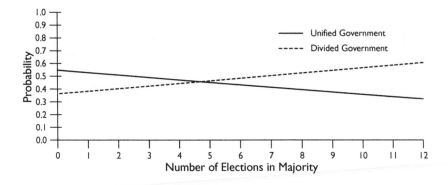

Independence

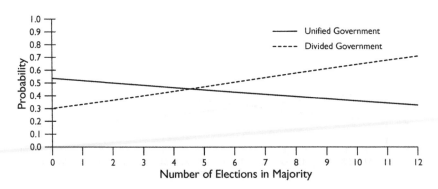

Specific Qualifications for Appointees

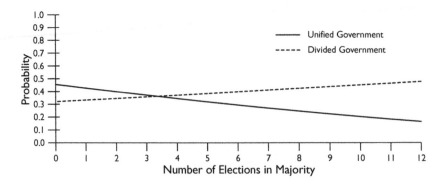

Governance by Commission

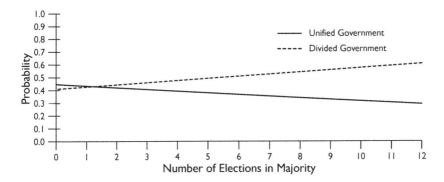

Fixed Terms

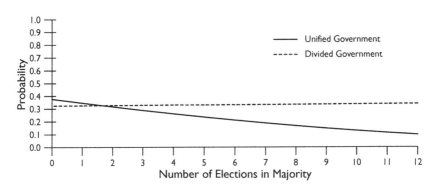

FIGURE 2.7   Impact of Presidential Approval Rating on the Probability of New Agencies Having Insulating Characteristics, 1946–97

Location Outside Cabinet

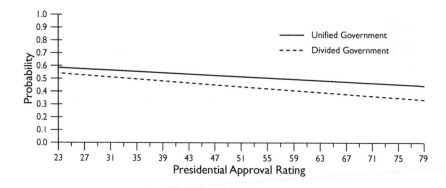

Independence

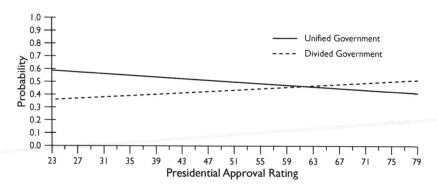

Specific Qualifications for Appointees

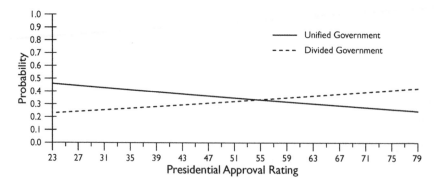

Governance by Commission

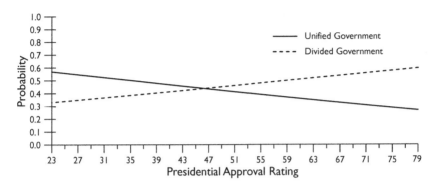

Fixed Terms

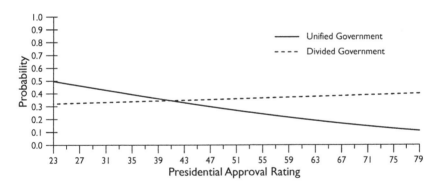

lation in unified government and increases it during periods of divided government.

This finding illustrates an important point that will be further developed in the next chapter. In each part of the agency design process Congress must anticipate the influence and preferences of the president. It is the president who will nominate public officials, propose budgets, and take administrative actions influencing the direction of new agencies. Models of political insulation that do not take into account the president ignore this important factor in the design of administrative agencies. The president's influence actually extends beyond that exercised after an agency has been created. Indeed, presidents exercise direct influence in the design of administrative agencies both in the legislative process and through the creation of administrative agencies through executive action.

DISCUSSION AND CONCLUSION

The quote from Gary King at the beginning the chapter suggested that the presidency (and bureaucracy) literature is one of the last bastions of non-quantitative research in American politics. This is not something that needs to characterize the study of the presidency or the bureaucracy. Both quantitative and qualitative research methods can fruitfully be brought to bear on empirical claims about the executive politics. The purpose of the preceding quantitative analysis is not to give artificial scientific legitimacy to my explanation of agency design and presidential influence. Rather, the quantitative analysis of agency design is intended to show how there are regularities in the agency design process across different instances and that understanding these broader processes takes us a long way toward understanding individual cases.

In particular, the quantitative analysis suggested that disagreements between the president and Congress can increase the probability that a new agency will be insulated, provided that Congress is strong enough. Who the president is and who the president will be have a substantial impact on member calculations. Models of political insulation that do not take into account the president ignore this important factor in the design of administrative agencies.

This chapter has focused on agency creation in Congress and how presidents benefit from having more partisans in Congress and from Congress's inability to come to agreement when a significant number oppose the president. The president's influence in agency decision making extends to other formal and informal presidential powers, however. The president has unique means of influence in both the legislative and administrative arenas. Indeed, I have examined only those agencies created by statute thus far, but more than one-half of all agencies created in the United States since 1946 were created by administrative action of one type or another, from executive and departmental orders to reorganization plans. Presidents use existing constitutional and statutory authority to create agencies that Congress did not ask for or necessarily condone, and they create these agencies in such a way that the agencies maximize presidential influence.

3

Presidents and the Politics of Agency Design

> Where one stands depends upon where one sits.
> —*Miles's Law*

In 1971 Gerald Ford, then a Republican member of Congress from Michigan, voted for a House bill creating an independent consumer agency. The new agency was going to monitor the affairs of government on behalf of consumers and intervene as litigants and participants in administrative actions on behalf of consumers. The proposal for the new agency was based upon the belief that business and industry, well equipped with high-paid lobbyists and resources, exercised undue influence over government policy to the detriment of consumers, a large and diffuse constituency. Similar bills passed in the House of Representatives in 1973 and 1974, only to die by Senate filibuster. Consumer advocates, buoyed by the election of a younger, more liberal Congress in 1974, pushed even harder for the new agency in 1975, and a measure creating such an agency passed both chambers. President Ford, however, stated in 1975 that he no longer supported the idea for the new independent agency and threatened to use his veto to back up his opposition. He proposed instead that all cabinet departments create what he called "consumer representation" plans that would create in-house consumer representatives. Ford's veto threat was sufficient to kill the proposal for the year.

Ford's change of heart about the wisdom of a new independent consumer agency coincided with his move from the House of Representatives to the White House. He is an excellent example of how the incentives of presidents are different from those of members of Congress and how much influence presidents can have over the design of administrative agencies.

A close examination of the historical record reveals a general pattern of presidential opposition to insulated political structures. Harold Seidman (1998) argues that presidents stand alone in opposition to the centrifugal tendencies in Congress and suggests that presidents are more or less successful in their endeavor to the degree they are able to grasp the political and strategic use of organizational structure. The Office of Management and Budget (OMB) (formerly the Bureau of the Budget) is also a source of presidential institutional memory. The OMB has historically sought to increase presidential influence and control (Peterson 1985). It is the locus of administrative management in the executive establishment.

Over time presidents, supported by the OMB and the various presidential commissions on administrative management, have both opposed congressional attempts to insulate new administrative agencies and actively sought to reorganize the bureaucracy to make it more amenable to presidential influence. Presidents have created a more hierarchical and responsive bureaucracy by influencing the legislative process, by actively proposing reorganization plans, and by unilaterally designing administrative structures.[1]

Presidents have historically opposed insulation in the executive branch. Like other actors, however, presidents act within a strategic context and are influenced by ideological considerations. Their proposals and actions are shaped by what is politically feasible given the preferences of Congress, the actions of bureaucrats, and the decisions of judges.[2] If presidents must choose between no agency and an agency that is more insulated than they prefer, they often will accept the proposal for the insulated agency.

Presidential behavior is also tempered by ideological considerations. In those circumstances when presidents acquiesce to insulation, the type of insulation they propose may vary based upon ideological predispositions and the relative impact that political insulation will have on Congress vis-à-vis the president. Republican presidents, for example, seem to favor government corporations more than Democratic presidents do because of their similarity to private sector organizations. In dismantling the Office of Economic Opportunity, for example, President Nixon proposed that the legal services component of the office be parceled off into a new government corporation, the Legal Services Corporation. President Bush, for example, proposed a Resolution Trust Corporation in 1989 off budget as a means of eliminating Congressional budget oversight.

The difference between the incentives of legislators and those of the president would not matter if the president had no means of influencing the design of administrative agencies. We have already seen how presidents get the types of structures they prefer when a substantial number of members share their policy preferences or when Congress cannot congeal to oppose presidential control, but presidents have other advantages in the agency design process. Presidential influence in the agency design process derives fundamentally from advantages related to presidents' constitutional position: their legislative power of the veto, their position as chief executive, and their position as a unitary actor. As Ford's example demonstrates, presidents exert substantial influence in the legislative process that creates agencies. They also have substantial discretionary authority as the constitutionally empowered executive and recipient of delegated authority to create agencies by executive action. Since 1946 more than one-half of all administrative agencies listed in the *United States Government Manual* have been created by executive action, namely reorganization plans, executive orders, or orders issued by department secretaries or agency heads.

HOW PRESIDENTS OPPOSE INSULATION

The modern president is frequently referred to as the "chief legislator" because of his influence in Congress. This influence in Congress is employed to influence the design of administrative agencies directly and to increase the amount of authority delegated by Congress. The veto is the president's most important source of legislative influence. Members of Congress must negotiate with the president on all important legislation because they can rarely garner the two-thirds majority necessary to override a veto. Presidents have used the veto or the threat of the veto to force Congress to change legislative proposals creating new agencies. President Truman vetoed Congress's initial proposal of a National Science Foundation because it was insulated from direct presidential control by two levels of administrative commissions. President Eisenhower vetoed a special coal research bill in 1959 because it vested authority in a new independent commission rather than the existing Bureau of Mines. President Johnson vetoed a bill creating an independent

Federal Maritime Administration because he believed responsibility for traffic on the nation's waterways belonged in the Department of Transportation. President Carter vetoed a bill creating an independent tourism administration because he favored incorporating tourism programs into the Commerce Department's International Trade Administration.

In most cases, however, the president's threat of a veto is enough to influence Congress to change the design of an administrative agency in accordance with the president's wishes. President Reagan's threat to veto a bill in 1988 creating a new Nuclear Safety Agency outside the Department of Energy resulted in its demise. In 1998 President Clinton threatened to veto a bill creating an Office of Religious Persecution Monitoring in the Executive Office of the President. He opposed creating a new bureaucracy separate from existing State Department and National Security Council bureaucracies and provisions mandating punitive sanctions against countries that have records of religious persecution. The eventual legislation that passed created a new Office of Religious Persecution Monitoring within the State Department bureaucracy and lacked the mandatory sanctions provision of the initial legislation.

Presidents have advantages in Congress stemming from their other formal constitutional powers. Presidents, first, are the chief executive. This provides them both informational advantages and advantages stemming from their ability to act first and force Congress to respond. In the same way that a CEO can exercise significant influence over the decisions of a board of directors, presidents exercise influence over members of Congress. The administrative officials testifying before Congress are usually first and foremost agents of the president. They clear their testimony before Congress with either the Office of Management and Budget or the White House. The president and his subordinates have the advantages that accrue to any agent in a principal-agent relationship. They have more information about agency policies, budgets, resources, and strategy. They can use this information to their advantage, justifying the creation of new agencies or forestalling congressional action.

Being chief executive also implies that presidents can act more quickly than Congress. It is difficult for Congress to come to agreement and pass legislation. The process of building a coalition to ensure passage of legislation is time-consuming, difficult, and fraught with obstacles. Action by the president, on the other hand, is not subject to these types of constraints. Acting with independent constitutional authority and authority delegated to the president over time, the president and his subordinates can act with the stroke of a pen and force Congress to respond (see Howell 2000; Moe and Howell 1998; Moe and Wilson 1994). Presidents often exploit the difficulties of legislative action by unilaterally enacting policies that garner the support of at least a third of the members or that will be unlikely to garner a successful congressional response. Ford's proposal for consumer action plans was just this type of action. It was enough of a response from the administration to derail stronger legislation.

These advantages are perhaps greatest in foreign policy, where the president exercises independent constitutional authority over foreign affairs and maintains the largest informational advantage over Congress (Canes-Wrone et al. 1999).[3] The president's ability to set policy by controlling troop training, troop movements, and military readiness, and his ability to initiate or refuse diplomatic relations and negotiate treaties, has no equivalent in domestic policy. In addition, although the president can bring to bear the resources of the entire State Department staff to bargain with Congress over the organization of foreign policy bureaucracy, for example, Congress must rely mainly on its committee staff, interest groups, and information provided by those same administrative agencies. Often presidents and their political appointees are the main providers of information to Congress. They can provide information in a manner that leads members to conclude that presidential policy is correct. In addition, when members of Congress have less information about the day-to-day workings of agencies and their policies, budgets, and programs, it is more difficult for them to publicly criticize and justify opposition to the president's preferences over structure and policy, giving presidents a significant advantage (Brody 1991).

There is disagreement as to whether the president's advantages in foreign policy derive more from his constitutional foreign policy powers or from the underlying institutional advantages of the chief executive.[4] The modern president's foreign policy powers, while formidable, were not necessarily intended by the Founders (see, e.g., Fisher 2000). The public good nature of national defense has led presidents to aggrandize power in this area and Congress to defer. Indeed, the president's control over information, his ability to act first, sometimes in secret, and his natural advantages over public opinion in foreign policy make it very difficult for Congress to constrain presidents. Members have neither the incentive nor the ability that they do in domestic policy, and the courts have been reticent to intervene in foreign policy or political questions, particularly when the two branches are in agreement.

Finally, the president's position as unitary head of state and the only nationally elected political official provides him substantial influence with members of Congress by virtue of his visibility and public esteem (Canes-Wrone and DeMarchi 2002; Rivers and Rose 1985). The public stature of presidents associated with the office and the personal approval that can come with it give presidents advantages in bargaining. Presidents have the ability to dispense rewards to members of Congress, particularly members of their own party. These rewards range from invitations to White House social gatherings to campaigning and intervening with the bureaucracy on a member's behalf. Popular presidents have resources that allow them to, in the language of some authors, "buy the votes" of members of Congress, particularly those members whose preferences are relatively close to their own. Presidential resources increase as presidents demonstrate popularity with the public, because members perceive more political benefit from being associated with a powerful president (Canes-Wrone and DeMarchi 2002). Members of the president's party hope to benefit from the coattails of a popular president.

The fact that presidents are popularly held responsible for the functioning of the entire government is a two-edged sword. In cases where they are perceived as successful, members of Congress are more likely to listen and go along. In cases where presidents are unpopular, even their partisans are likely to distance themselves.

In sum, although presidents certainly benefit from having like-minded members of Congress serving or benefiting from a divided Congress, they also exercise influence in the legislative process through their use of the veto, their foreign policy powers, and their personal approval, all of which derive from their institutional position in our separation-of-powers system.

PRESIDENTIAL USE OF ADMINISTRATIVE DISCRETION

The formal power as chief executive provides the president another means of influencing the shape of the bureaucracy. Some type of executive action—executive order, departmental order, or reorganization plan—is responsible for over half of all agencies created in the United States since 1946.[5] Under what conditions will presidents want to create agencies by such means? Presidents would prefer to create agencies by statute as long as they have had influence in the agency's crafting. If presidents cannot get agencies created by statute in the manner they prefer, they often will create agencies by executive action. As such, the alternative to an agency created by executive action is often no agency at all or an agency that would have looked dramatically different from the one the president created. Historically, presidential attempts to respond to increased pressure for federal action on civil rights illustrate the first case.[6] President George W. Bush's creation of the Office of Homeland Security illustrates the second case.

Congressional Disability

The roots of presidential unilateral action and fair employment trace back to the 1941 Fair Employment Practices Committee. In response to threats from the National Association for the Advancement of Colored People and the Urban League to march on Washington in 1941, President Roosevelt issued Executive Order 8802. He issued Executive Order 9346 in 1943, when frustrated civil rights advocates threatened to march again. The orders established the Fair Employment Practices Committee (FEPC) and invested it with the responsibility of ensuring nondiscrimination in government contracts. Several bills were introduced to formally authorize the new FEPC in statute, but none made it out of committee.

In 1946, Richard Russell (D-Ga.) proposed legislation requiring congressional sanction of all monies for executive-created agencies that had been in existence for more than one year. This meant the end of the FEPC, since the president could not secure an appropriation for the controversial agency. In 1948, however, President Truman issued Executive Order 9880, creating a new Fair Employment Board to perform essentially the same functions as the FEPC except limited to federal government employees. Three years later Truman's Executive Order 10308 created the Government Committee on Contract Compliance (GCCC) to ensure nondiscrimination in government contracts.

Eisenhower extended Truman's GCCC, and President Kennedy issued Executive Order 10925 in 1961 to create the President's Committee on Equal Employment Opportunity.

Throughout this period, members of Congress introduced legislation to formally authorize these agencies created by executive action or to create others. The legislation they introduced could not survive the obstacle course of committee chairmen, rules committee votes, or filibusters. Apart from the limited successes of the 1957 and 1960 civil rights laws, Congress could not respond to civil rights concerns. Roosevelt, Truman, Eisenhower, and Kennedy all could have done more to ensure fair employment practices. What is equally true, however, is that presidents felt uniquely responsible to respond to public pressure and that the alternative to the fair employment agencies they created likely would have been no agencies and perhaps no action at all.

Presidential Preemption

In cases where Congress seems prepared to create agencies insulated from presidential control, presidents also executively create agencies to preempt congressional action. The Office of Homeland Security created in the aftermath of the September 11, 2001, terrorist attacks is a good example. On October 8, President Bush issued an executive order creating the Office of Homeland Security (OHS) to coordinate the administration's response to threats against domestic security. The office was charged with the responsibility of coordinating the more than fifty federal agencies with homeland security responsibilities, including the Federal Bureau of Investigation, the Department of Defense, the Coast Guard, the Border Patrol, and the Immigration and Naturalization Service (Becker and Sciolino 2001; Peters 2001). It was also charged with coordinating state and local responses to possible domestic threats. The president's actions helped him coordinate a domestic response to security threats but also forestalled more severe congressional action, which he opposed.

The OHS was not the only possible response by Congress or the president. In fact, on January 31, 2001, before the attacks, the U.S. Commission on National Security/21st Century, or the Hart-Rudman Commission, released its recommendations for the consolidation of a number of agencies with domestic security responsibilities (U.S. Commission on National Security 2001).

The commission proposed merging the Coast Guard, the Federal Emergency Management Agency, the Customs Service, and the Border Patrol into one National Homeland Security Agency with cabinet rank (Peters

2001). In March Representative Mac Thornberry (R-Tex.) proposed legislation to implement the commission's recommendations. In the aftermath of the September attacks, members of Congress quickly began to consider other variations of the commission's recommendations (McCutcheon 2001). Senator Joseph Lieberman (D-Conn.) and Representative Jane Harman (D-Calif.) both introduced bills to create a homeland security agency. Senator Bob Graham (D-Fla.) began working on legislation to officially authorize the new office.

The administration, however, sought to discourage these attempts directly through contacts and statements from the White House. President Bush invited a bipartisan group of legislators to the White House, where he asked them directly to hold off on legislation creating a new agency for homeland security (Koffler 2001). The White House feared that a new agency created by Congress might be ill considered and might limit the president's flexibility in responding. By creating the OHS by executive action, he forestalled what would likely have been a legislative response to the crisis. Creating the OHS satisfied enough members to derail any potential legislation, at least for a time. This gave the administration more time to consider whether they favored a new agency or the existing structure.

The Source of Presidential Authority

The president's ability to create agencies by executive action derives both from nondelegated constitutional authority and authority delegated by Congress. The president has used his constitutional or delegated authority in ways both consistent and inconsistent with congressional expectations and at times has used the ambiguity, conflict, and vagueness of Congress's various delegations of authority in ways inconsistent with congressional wishes. Consider the following examples of presidential unilateral action:

1. Constitutional *authority*. President Kennedy created the President's Committee on Equal Employment Opportunity by Executive Order 10925 in 1961. The committee, ostensibly created on the basis of the president's executive power in Article 2, was charged with enforcing nondiscrimination policies in federal government employment and government contractors. The committee forced firms to post nondiscrimination statements and file compliance reports, and it exhibited

the power to cancel contracts of businesses with histories of racial discrimination.

2. *Unanticipated use of delegated authority.* In 1969 Congress enacted the Economic Stabilization Act, which granted the president the authority to freeze certain wages and prices. The president responded by creating the Cost of Living Council, the Pay Board, and the Price Commission by executive order to carry out the controls he announced. However, Congress and organized labor interests complained about domination of the Pay Board by the White House and business interests and decisions rolling back union wage increases. Pro-labor members of Congress also criticized the Price Commission for what they perceived to be policies that did not place stringent enough limitations on profits. Congress subsequently passed legislation requiring Senate confirmation of the chairmen of the Pay Board and Price Commission.

3. Creative *use of vague statutes.* In 1961 the new Kennedy administration initiated the food stamp program under the authority of section 32 of Public Law 74-320 enacted in 1935. This law earmarked 30 percent of U.S. customs earnings to the Secretary of Agriculture to encourage exports, encourage domestic consumption, and increase farmers' purchasing power. The notoriously broad section had been used previously to finance export subsidies, support agricultural research, and purchase food surpluses for donation to school lunch and welfare programs. The Democratic Congress, over the objections of the Republican minority, eventually gave the program explicit statutory authority in 1964.[7]

Since 1946, forty-three new agencies, or 10 percent of all agencies created, were created by executive order. These include the National Security Agency, the Federal Emergency Management Agency, the Central Security Service, and the Domestic Policy Council.

In addition to agencies created directly by the president via executive order, the president's political appointees also create agencies. In such circumstances Congress has passed at one time or another legislation vesting authority for implementation of a specific program in a particular agency. Secretaries create, by their own initiative and at their own discretion, organizational units to implement legislation passed by Congress. These agencies are less directly attributable to presidential action but are nonetheless created within the purview and control of the White House and designed by executive actors who share the president's concern for centralization, hierarchy, and political control. For example, in 1952 Congress authorized $2 million for research on converting seawater into freshwater. In response, the secretary of interior created the Office of Saline Water to implement the new program. In 1954 the administrator of the Housing and Home Finance Agency created the Community Facilities Administration and the Urban Renewal Administration to implement legislation enacted by Congress. In 1984 the secretary of defense created the Strategic Defense Initiative Organization to implement the missile defense system pushed by President Reagan. Since 1946, some type of secretarial order created 41 percent of all new agencies listed in the *United States Government Manual.* The Occupational Health and Safety Administration, the Welfare Administration, and the Bureau of Alcohol, Tobacco, and Firearms are among the agencies created by department secretaries or agency heads.

In addition to agencies created by executive order or secretarial order, Congress has also frequently given presidents and their subordinates reorganization authority (Fisher 1998). Defense Secretary Robert McNamara used reorganization authority granted by Congress in 1958 to create the Defense Intelligence Agency and the Defense Supply Agency in 1961. Under the most common form of reorganization authority granted by Congress, presidents make reorganization proposals and submit them to Congress. If Congress fails either to alter or to negate the plans, they go into effect after a specified period of time. The type of congressional action (one-house veto, two-house veto, joint resolution) necessary to stop a reorganization plan and the length of time necessary to expire before a plan goes into effect have varied. The collective action problems described above make it difficult for Congress to respond to such presidential initiatives. It is difficult for party leadership to drum up support and interest and schedule votes within the short time window. Since the Supreme Court struck down the legislative veto in the *INS v. Chadha* (1983) decision, however, the president's reorganization authority has lapsed. Any president now wishing to reorganize the bureaucracy must pursue the reorganization directly through legislation. The Drug Enforcement Agency, the Office of Personnel Management, the Environmental Protection Agency, and the Federal Transit Administration were all created by reorganization plan.

CONGRESSIONAL RESPONSES

When an executive official creates a new agency, of course, Congress can pass legislation eliminating it, or legislators can simply refuse to appropriate money for its operations. However, in most circumstances it is difficult for Congress to pass legislation eliminating an agency, and Congress only rarely has refused appropriations to a new agency. The president's ability to create agencies by executive action gives members an opportunity to create agencies that might never be created through the legislative process.

Although this would appear to offend the sensibilities of Congress as an institution, Congress is not good at defending its institutional interests against presidential encroachment, particularly when a significant portion of the members support the president's actions. Because members of Congress are concerned primarily with reelection and the interests of their districts, they individually have very little incentive to protect the institutional interests of Congress. As Terry Moe and Scott Wilson (1994, 24) argue, "They are trapped in a prisoner's dilemma: while all might benefit if they could cooperate in defending Congress's power, there are strong incentives for each to free-ride if support for the collective good is politically costly to them as individuals." As a consequence, Congress can rarely respond to what many members view as an encroachment on congressional authority.

Even if a majority in Congress congeals to respond to the president's creation of a new agency, this does not guarantee its enactment. At each step of the way individual members of Congress sympathetic to the president's position can halt the progress of a piece of legislation. Individual senators can filibuster or place holds on legislation. Only a cloture vote of sixty senators can overcome a filibuster. The president can also veto such measures. To override a veto Congress must muster two-thirds majorities in both chambers of Congress. This is very difficult to do because presidential partisans usually far exceed the necessary one-third of legislature necessary to sustain a veto.

Over time Congress has developed some tools to overcome the advantages of presidential unilateral action, such as omnibus bills, closed rules, restrictive appropriations language, and the whip system, but these tools have not eliminated the presidential influence exerted from acting first and forcing Congress to respond.

Appropriations

Congress also exerts substantial influence over the creation of agencies by virtue of its appropriations power. As will be discussed below, however, Congress rarely refuses new agencies funds, and when it has succeeded in terminating or seriously restricting presidentially created agencies, the president has created new agencies in their place to perform the same functions.

Using Existing Accounts

The Russell Amendment, passed in response to President Roosevelt's unilateral creation of the Fair Employment Practices Commission, states the following:

> No part of any appropriation or fund made available . . . shall be allotted or made available to, or used to pay the expenses of, any agency or instrumentality including those established by Executive order after such an agency or instrumentality has been in existence for more than one year, if the Congress has not appropriated any money specifically for such agency or instrumentality or specifically authorized the expenditure of funds by it. (58 *STAT* 387)

The statute appears to require new agencies to receive either a statutory authorization or a specific appropriation by Congress. The amendment, however, has been interpreted in practice to require only that a new agency's existence be justified in larger budget presentations.[8] New agencies do not have to receive specific authorization from Congress.

Of course, Congress must appropriate all money spent by the executive. Smaller agencies, bureaus, and offices can be created and funded in their first year with money previously appropriated by Congress. The budget is divided into spending accounts that are assigned specific numbers. Money cannot be legally transferred among these accounts. The size and specificity of these accounts vary, however. Some accounts are quite large, whereas others are quite small. These accounts also vary according to how many restraints, formal and informal, Congress places on how the money is to be spent. Agencies present their budget requests to Congress supported by documentation, evidence, and explanations about how appropriations will be spent, and Congress determines the level of appropriation based upon these presentations.

The degree of specificity statutorily and informally can vary from a lump sum with few restrictions to an itemized accounting to the minute detail.

In accounts where Congress has not placed a number of restrictions, executive branch officials have the ability to spend appropriated funds according to their discretion. So in cases where Congress has delegated new authority to the president or his subordinates, they have the ability to create new agencies or bureaus and use vague appropriations to fund them. For example, President Kennedy funded the Peace Corps from a contingency fund in foreign assistance appropriations during its first year.[9] Contingency funds had been routinely included in annual appropriations for emergencies and unforeseen circumstances.

Executive branch officials also have a limited ability to reprogram funds budgeted for one purpose in a single account to another program or activity funded from the same program account. Most limitations on appropriated funds are informal, derived from good faith understanding between congressional committees and agencies that agencies will spend money in accordance with their itemized budget requests. As Louis Fisher (1975, 73) explains, "If agencies violate that trust and abuse their discretionary powers, they face the prospect the next year of budget cutbacks, restrictive language, and line-item appropriations." Still, these "understandings" are not always honored, and Congress, recognizing the need for discretion, has created a mechanism for "reprogramming" funds within a single account. Most such mechanisms require that the executive branch notify and receive the approval of the relevant congressional committees to perform such a reprogramming. The amount of money necessary to trigger a notification varies from agency to agency. In some cases as much as 15 percent of a budget account can be reprogrammed without congressional notification.

Agencies created by executive action can be created and funded in their first year by presidents according to the preceding pattern. Presidents, however, must continue to secure funding for these agencies in subsequent years. In a few cases, presidents seek to continue funding new agencies through preexisting program accounts. In these cases, the Russell Amendment mandates that presidents include explicit justification for the new agency in budget presentations made before the appropriate congressional committee the next year.

Obtaining a New Account

In most cases, however, presidents seek a new account for a new agency. Presidents usually receive the appropriations they request for the new agencies for a number of reasons. First, it is hard for Congress to refuse to fund a new agency because it is usually performing some function that Congress wants performed. In many cases Congress delegates authority to the president or to an agency with the knowledge that the executive official might create a new organizational unit to implement legislators' policy objectives. In either case, if Congress refuses to fund the agency, it can disrupt the enforcement and implementation of statutes it has enacted. Truman's Loyalty Review Board is a good example. In 1947, in response to congressional agitation, President Truman appointed a Temporary Commission on Employee Loyalty to recommend action to ensure loyalty among government employees. In response to the commission's recommendations, Truman created the Loyalty Review Board by executive order. The Republican majority in Congress attempted to establish its own version of the board by statute. Although the bill passed the House, the Senate never acted on it. Majority members had held up funds for Truman's Loyalty Review Board but ultimately funded it when their alternative could not pass Congress.

Second, in some cases a new agency exists and has been up and running for up to a year by the time Congress has a chance to decide upon its appropriations. The new agency is presented as a fait accompli supported by the administration, the agency, and friends in Congress. The creation of the Peace Corps is a good example. In the 1950s Senator Hubert Humphrey (D-Minn.) and Representative Henry S. Reuss (D-Wis.) first proposed the idea of sending volunteers overseas for aid and for training and education. Humphrey and Reuss introduced legislation in 1960 to study the practicality of such a program. Republicans rejected the proposal as a "juvenile experiment," and Richard Nixon claimed that its volunteers would just be seeking to escape the draft. Once in office, Kennedy bypassed the legislative process and created the Peace Corps by executive order. Congressional Republicans decried his actions, arguing that the Peace Corps was too expensive, was of little value, and its creation by executive order was an abuse of presidential power. By the time Congress acted on the legislation giving statutory basis for the Peace Corps, the Corps had 362 Washington employees and 600 volunteers at work in eight countries (Whitnah 1983). Republican attempts to defund the agency were defeated by program and administration supporters in Congress.

Finally, presidential attempts to fund new agencies are shielded by the larger budget process. The budget is large and complex, and most of the debate about its contents focuses on incremental changes to existing accounts. Herbert Kaufman (1976, 7) writes,

> The budget is now so huge that Congress and its subdivisions could not, even if they were inclined to, treat it as a totally new document each year. Rather, the record of expenditures in the recent past is taken as a base, and attention is focused on whether to exceed the base by some fraction . . . , reduce it by some fraction . . . , or leave it as it is. Total elimination of funds for an established agency or even massive slashes approaching total elimination are unknown, for all practical purposes.

In most cases new agencies do not arise de novo to carry out a new federal government function. Rather, the new larger agencies combine preexisting related activities into one large, functionally related agency. The Drug Enforcement Agency, for example, combined four distinct drug law enforcement agencies. In most cases, the money for enforcement of the disparate programs already exists in separate program accounts. Much of what is involved is the reallocation of appropriations to a new program account for the new agency. Presidents present new proposed agencies in the budget in italics with their proposed reallocation of appropriations. All of the budget estimates and proposals for marginal increases and decreases in the president's budget are made with reference to the new organizational arrangements. If Congress prefers the old structure, it must determine how the president's estimates, increments, and proposals relate to the old accounts.

These types of overt conflicts are rare, however, and usually are resolved in negotiations prior to presidential actions. However, when Congress has attempted to defund a presidential agency, presidents have responded by creating new agencies to perform similar functions. When Congress refused to fund President Roosevelt's FEPC, Truman set up the Fair Employment Board within the Civil Service Commission to serve the same function (Morgan 1970). In response to President Reagan's subjection of all new regulations to cost-benefit analysis beginning in 1981, Congress attempted in 1986 to defund the agency responsible, the Office of Information and Regulatory Affairs (OIRA). After extracting what members believed to be concessions from the OMB and the White House, Congress relented in its attempts. Ambiguities in the agreement, however, led to continued conflict between the legislative and executive branches over the regulatory review practices of the OMB. President Bush consequently transferred OIRA's functions to Vice-President Quayle's Council on Competitiveness. In 1992, the House voted to delete funding for the salaries of staffers on the council, but the Senate restored the funds when President Bush threatened a veto (see Fisher 1998, 36–39).

What is clear from the preceding discussion and examples is that presidents use their formal and informal powers to influence the legislative process and to create administrative agencies through executive action. Presidents use their legislative power of the veto, their position as chief executive, and their position as a unitary actor to gain an advantage in the struggle over the design of the administrative state. When there is a large number of presidential partisans in Congress and presidents have high approval or presidents are acting in foreign affairs, they are likely to have more success in Congress. His advantage as chief executive and unitary actor provides the president with opportunities to create agencies that Congress could not create or did not anticipate, and presidents design these agencies so that they maximize executive control. Congress has a more difficult time responding to such actions when it is more difficult for members to reach agreement.

A STRUGGLE BETWEEN BRANCHES

Early in his tenure as president Gerald Ford was able to use his veto power to ward off the creation of a new independent consumer agency. What we witnessed in Ford's opposition to the independent consumer agency reflects a broader truth about the role of presidents in the design of administrative agencies. Presidents are not like legislators. They generally oppose insulation and exercise influence over the eventual design of administrative agencies by influencing the legislative process and through the administrative discretion inherent in their role as chief executive.

A president benefits from formal powers like the veto power, his role as chief executive, and his role as unitary head of state. Ford used the threat of a veto to stop the consumer agency legislation. He used authority derived from his role as chief executive to propose consumer action plans as an alternative. Ford's attempt to substitute consumer action plans in the existing departments for a new consumer agency was an attempt to derail congressional action by unilateral action. Ultimately, his action was sufficient to convince a veto-sustaining coalition that enough was being done to protect consumers. It gave members cover to show they were sympathetic to consumer interests.

All presidents have strategic advantages arising from their constitutional position in our separation-of-powers system. One of the most important of these is the ability not only to forestall legislative action with unilateral action but to create agencies by unilateral action. Presidents do so either to act when Congress cannot or to preempt congressional action. Presidents, using constitutional or delegated authority, can act and force Congress to respond. In many cases Congress does not want to respond, agreeing more or less with the president's decision in principle if not in the details. In other cases, Congress cannot respond because members cannot get legislation through Congress or withhold appropriations nimbly enough to counteract the president's action.

Although Ford was successful opposing an independent consumer agency, he did oversee the creation of the Federal Election Commission, the Commodity Futures Trading Commission, and the Nuclear Regulatory Commission, three independent regulatory commissions. Ford also vetoed more significant legislation than any other modern president. As the unelected successor to Richard Nixon, Ford was a weak president. He had very little influence in the heavily Democratic Congress, no control over the legislative agenda, and deteriorating public approval. His only recourse was to negate the legislation being passed in Congress. Ford was weak because he faced a large opposition majority with both the incentive and the ability to go toe-to-toe with the succession president. Ford's case illustrates how agency design fundamentally boils down to a struggle between branches. The strength or weakness of each branch will influence the chances that a new agency will be amenable to presidential direction or removed from his control.

$$4$$

Testing the Role of Presidents: Presidential Administrative Influence

> I just—you are going to go ahead and do it then? So this authorization is really, if it comes, it comes, but if it doesn't, you are going ahead unauthorized?
>
> —Representative Charles Taylor (R-N.C.)

On Earth Day, April 22, 1993, President Clinton announced plans to create a new National Biological Survey (NBS) within the Department of the Interior. The NBS was going to gather the information and technological resources necessary to manage the nation's biological resources. The NBS became fully operational the following November after Congress appropriated $163 million for its operations. Republicans like Charles Taylor were not happy about the NBS's creation. They stated their concerns that the NBS would become a vehicle for enforcement of the Endangered Species Act. They worried that federal agents would collect data on private property and perhaps discover endangered species that would lower the values of land-owners' property.

Congressional attempts to create the NBS by statute failed, but creation by department order was sufficient. Once it received appropriations as part of the larger Interior Department appropriations, it began operations. The NBS is an example of the hundreds of agencies created by executive rather than legislative action. Many executive-created agencies are created with the implicit approval of Congress. Others, like the NBS, are created over the objections of a significant number of members. Some are supported in principle by legislators but opposed in practice because of objections to specific details of their design and policies.

Since 1946, the president or his subordinates have created more than *one-half* of all administrative agencies created in the United States.[1] Research that assumes that Congress creates all administrative agencies tells, at most, only half the story. Thus far I have focused mainly on agencies created through the legislative process. In this chapter I take a closer look at executive-created agencies. Through an analysis of the NBS case in more detail and quantitative analysis of agencies created by executive action since 1946, I show how agencies created by administrative actions are less likely to be insulated from presidential control. I also show that Congress does not dominate the politics of creating agencies by executive action. Indeed, the number of administrative agencies created by administrative actors is determined, in part, by the strength of the president and Congress's inability to pass legislation.

Ultimately, presidents gain an advantage in the politics of agency design by their ability to create agencies unilaterally. They take advantage of Congress's inability to act to create agencies administratively, agencies that differ significantly from those created through the legislative process.

AGENCIES CREATED BY EXECUTIVE ACTION

Since 1946, the U.S. government has created 437 agencies. The president or his subordinates have created 248, or 57 percent, of these by administrative action. Executive-created agencies are generally smaller than legislatively created agencies. About one-half of all executive-created agencies have a separate line in the budget, compared with 70 percent for legislatively created agencies. The average budget for an executive-created agency at its inception is about $2 billion in 1992 dollars. The average budget for a legislatively created agency at its creation is $4.13 billion, or about twice that of executive-created agencies. These budget numbers are partly inflated by war agencies and grant-making agencies like the Office of Revenue Sharing, but executive-created agencies, although smaller, still have substantial budgets. Agencies created by executive action are also less likely to get noticed by contemporaneous reports of legislative politics. About 30 percent of all executive-created agencies, compared with 60 percent for legislatively created agencies, were mentioned in *Congress and the Nation* during the period when they were created.[2]

Not surprisingly, these agencies are much less likely to be insulated from presidential control. On the five-category measure of agency location, the median value for agencies created by executive action is 2, indicating location in a cabinet agency. Legislatively created agencies also have a median value of 2. The average score, however, is 2.2 for executive-created agencies and 2.8 for legislatively created agencies, a statistically significant difference (p < .00, 430 df).

Agencies created by executive action are also significantly less likely to be created as independent agencies. Although some, like the National Intelligence Authority, the U.S. Information Agency, and the Federal Emergency Management Agency, were created by executive action and are independent, they appear to be the exception during the 1946–97 period. Only 11 percent of all agencies created by executive action are independent, compared with 36 percent for statutorily created agencies (p < .00, 427 df).

Although presidents frequently meet their need for advice and study through commission-governed advisory bodies, they are less likely to create agencies with nonadvisory functions that are governed by boards or commissions. Some of the exceptions are the Foreign Claims Settlement Commission and the Government Patents Board. However, boards or commissions govern only 13 percent of all agencies created by executive action, compared with 44 percent of legislatively created agencies (p < .00, 426 df).

Not only do presidents rarely favor commission governance, but they also rarely endorse fixed terms for political appointees. No federal agency created by executive order or departmental order during the 1946–97 period has fixed terms for political appointees. Political appointees who serve for fixed terms govern only three agencies initiated by presidents in reorganization plans, including the Federal Maritime Commission and the Federal Labor Relations Authority. One reason why presidents eschew fixed terms in agencies created by executive order or departmental order is that they are not usually a credible constraint on presidential influence. Since he created the agency by executive action, the president could terminate or alter the agency by executive action later if it did something he did not approve, making the guarantee of nonreprisal noncredible.

Presidents have, however, purposefully limited their influence over appointments by adding specific qualifications to political appointees. Although 40 percent of agencies created by legislation have some form of limiting qualification for political appointees, only 8 percent of executive-created agencies have such limitations. Presidents have never imposed party-balancing limitations on a commission they have created.

In sum, agencies created by executive orders, departmental orders, or reorganization plans are smaller than agencies created by statute. They also are less likely to be noticed by congressional reporters. This is not to suggest, however, that they are not important. On the contrary, these agencies employ thousands of people, have substantial budgets at their inception, and are important enough to be listed in the *United States Government Manual*. The president or his subordinates have created some of the most important administrative agencies of the postwar period. The president created the National Security Agency and the Peace Corps by executive order. His subordinate political appointees created the Occupational Safety and Health Administration, the National Marine Fisheries Service, and the Pension and Welfare Benefits Administration. Reorganization plans created the Department of Health, Education, and Welfare; the Environmental Protection Agency; and the Office of Personnel Management. Importantly, the character of executive-created agencies overwhelmingly indicates that presidents rarely create agencies that are insulated from their control. Executive-created agencies are substantially less likely to be insulated on all five indicators of insulation. As such, focusing only on legislatively created agencies likely mischaracterizes the politics of agency design and underestimates the influence of presidents.

One plausible explanation for the design of executive-created agencies is that Congress delegates authority for executive-created agencies only when members prefer that the agency be uninsulated. Such a statement assumes, however, that Congress has one unified preference and can perfectly delegate its authority, anticipate how it will be used, and easily respond to presidential use of delegated authority that is inconsistent with congressional intent. It also assumes that Congress reevaluates in each session how much delegated authority the current president should have. None of these assumptions is true. Presidents frequently rely upon their supporters in Congress to fend off attempts in Congress to oppose agencies or measures they have initiated with executive action. Presidents and their subordinates also continue to use vague and conflicting statutes and old delegations of authority in ways that are inconsistent with the preferences of many members of Congress. Finally, Congress is afflicted with collective action problems. Passing any legislation is difficult, and gathering a coalition to respond to a presidential unilateral action is even more difficult. Many members invariably support the president's actions and will oppose attempts to override him in Congress.

DOES CONGRESS DICTATE THE CREATION OF EXECUTIVE-CREATED AGENCIES? THE CASE OF THE NATIONAL BIOLOGICAL SERVICE

> I'm asking the Interior Department to create a national biological survey to help us protect endangered species and, just as importantly, to help the agricultural and biotechnical industries of our country identify new sources of food, fiber and medication.
> —President Clinton, April 21, 1993

President Clinton announced plans for the creation of a National Biological Survey on Earth Day, April 22, 1993.[3] Clinton's hope was to create a unified biological science bureau within the Department of the Interior mostly to carry out previously existing but fragmented responsibilities.

Supporters of the idea, including Interior Secretary Bruce Babbitt, claimed that a single science agency within the Interior Department would be more efficient and effective than existing fragmented efforts (Corn 1995). Many of the functions of the new bureau could be traced back to the Bureau of Biological Survey created in the Agriculture Department in 1885. However, since that time the task of gathering the information and technologies necessary for management of the nation's biological resources had been dispersed among a number of different bureaus within the Interior Department and outside agencies.[4] Three external studies, one by the Office of Management and Budget in 1980, another by the Carnegie Commission in 1992, and one commissioned by Secretary Babbitt and conducted by the National Research Council in February 1993, recommended that the Interior Department consolidate its science programs. The fragmentation of biological research functions, they suggested, lead to duplication, piecemeal responses to complex problems, and unnecessary expense (Corn 1995).

The NBS Gets Its Start

Citing authority from Reorganization Plan 3 of 1950, Babbitt issued order 3173 to create the NBS five months later, on September 29, 1993.[5] The stated purpose of the NBS was to "gather, analyze, and disseminate the biological information necessary for the sound stewardship of our Nation's natural resources and to foster understanding of biological systems and the benefits they provide to society" (U.S. Department of Interior 1993). The new bureau assumed the biological research, monitoring, and information transfer functions previously performed by seven other Interior Department bureaus (U.S. Department of Interior 1994). The order transferred close to seventeen hundred scientists, mathematicians, and curators to the service, primarily from the Fish and Wildlife Service.

Although the order creating the NBS was issued on September 29, the NBS did not become fully operational until November 11, when Congress appropriated funds for its operation.[6] By law, all new agencies must be authorized by Congress within two years of their creation to receive appropriations. Congress never formally authorized the NBS. Instead, the solicitor of the Department of Interior and members of Congress reasoned that the inclusion of the NBS in the department's budget justifications was sufficient for it to receive appropriations.[7] Babbitt requested $179 million for its operations for FY 1994, $40 million more than had been appropriated for these functions in FY 1993 (U.S. House 1993b, 15). Congress eventually appropriated $163 million for the NBS to begin operations, $140 million transferred from other bureaus and $24 million in new funds.

Congress Tries to Create the NBS by Statute

During the summer of 1993, sympathetic members of Congress introduced HR 1845 and a companion Senate bill, S1110, to give the NBS formal statutory authority. They introduced the legislation shortly after the president's announcement in April and concurrent with the Department of Interior's plans to create the agency administratively. The bills sought to establish the NBS permanently, providing for a director experienced in the biological sciences appointed by the president with the advice and consent of the Senate. The administration lobbied for the legislation.

Two congressional committees held hearings during the summer of 1993 to craft a legislative version of the agency palatable to a majority of members. Indeed, congressional Democrats generally supported the idea of a national biological survey. A number of Republicans and conservative Democrats, however, opposed authorization. They worried about the NBS's activities regarding private land, the reliability of data collected by "liberal" volunteers, the potential impact findings of new endangered species would have on the property values of landowners, and the possibility that the NBS's activities would lead to new regulation.[8]

Land rights, farmers, and "wise-use" groups mobilized a campaign in July and August to stop the NBS legislation. Representative Don Young (R-Alaska) declared that the NBS was part of "a socialist agenda to make sure Big Brother, big Government, controls all and everyone." Representative Bill Emerson (R-Mo.) charged, "This National Biological Survey is nothing more than an attack on the principles of the fifth amendment of the U.S. Constitution."[9]

The House passed HR 1845 on October 26, 1993, by a vote of 255 to 165 after accepting two amendments that watered down the initial bill. The first amendment outlawed the use of volunteers to perform survey activities, and the second mandated that the NBS get written permission before entering private property. The Senate never took action.

The administration, although disappointed with the outcome, was prepared to continue the NBS as an independent bureau without statutory authorization. It succeeded in obtaining appropriations even though it had failed to in its attempts to get authorizing legislation. Secretary Babbitt's statement in congressional testimony makes this clear:

> Mr. Taylor: I think you probably have the legal authority (to obtain appropriations without statutory authorization). I just—you are going to go ahead and do it then? So this authorization is really, if it comes, it comes, but if it doesn't, you are going ahead unauthorized?
>
> Secretary Babbitt: Subject to authority from the Appropriation Committees in the final appropriation process, the answer is, yes. (U.S. House 1993a, 41)

The NBS continued as an independent bureau within the Interior Department in basically the form dictated by the departmental order rather than the House bill. The director did not require Senate confirmation, no limits were placed on who the president or secretary could appoint, and with one exception there were no additional statutory restrictions on the director or agency. Having failed to limit the NBS in authorizing legislation, the NBS's opponents in the House were able to win compromise language in the Interior Department and Related Agencies Appropriations Bill, requiring that NBS officials gain written permission before venturing onto private land, one of the two amendments accepted for the House version of the NBS authorization bill (*Congressional Quarterly Almanac* 1993, 627).

The case of the NBS illustrates some of the advantages of unilateral action to create administrative agencies. By creating the NBS administratively, President Clinton was able to create an agency that would not have been created by legislation. Not only was he able to create something that he could not get in legislation, but also he was able to design it the way he wanted. He could appoint its director without confirmation, and its employees had fewer constraints on how they conducted their operations. If Congress had created the agency, it would have attached qualifications to whom he could appoint, would have required Senate confirmation, and would likely have added restrictions on NBS use of volunteers and mandated peer review for data collection activities.

The NBS Succumbs to Its Opponents

Like most other federal agencies, the NBS continued to grow after its creation. By 1995, the service employed nineteen hundred persons and operated fifteen science centers, ninety field stations, and fifty-four cooperative research units. Its budget had grown steadily. Although the NBS continued to grow, it was still opposed by the coalition that stalled its formal authorization. Only now that coalition had obtained a majority in Congress after the 1994 midterm elections. Part of the Republicans' "Contract with America" specifically called for the abolition of the NBS. Republicans and conservative Democrats such as W. J. "Billy" Tauzin (D-La.) and Gary Condit (D-Calif.), unhappy with the NBS from the start, continued to publicly criticize the agency and seek its termination.[10] Representative Don Young (R-Alaska) criticized government scientists as "federal goons" and Representative Wayne Allard (R-Colo.) petitioned Speaker Newt Gingrich (R-Ga.) to help him abolish the NBS.

Within weeks of assuming power, the Republican-lead House Budget Committee received testimony from witnesses advising the House to abolish the NBS (Cushman 1995; Reich 1995). Budget committee chairman John Kasich (R-Ohio) favored the elimination of most of the Interior Department's science budget, of which the NBS was a part. The House version of the FY 1996 appropriations bill for the Interior Department included a provision eliminating the NBS. The Senate version of the bill only cut the NBS's budget and proposed to rename the agency while allowing it to continue its independent existence. In conference, however, the House version won out. President Clinton subsequently vetoed the bill.

Secretary Babbitt defended the department's science programs, lauding their contribution and decrying what he called "the notion that science is a problem, that we'd be better off without knowledge" (Reich 1995). He said he hoped to "provoke a tidal wave of indignation" over threats to the Interior Department's science budget. In perhaps a foreshadowing of things to come, however, Babbitt acknowledged that if Congress eliminated any of the three Interior Department science agencies, it would be difficult for the president to respond. "Because such decisions could come in a budget bill of $1.5 trillion, it would not be easy for the president to veto them" (Reich 1995).

Congress reintroduced the Interior Appropriations Bill later that year as part of a larger omnibus appropriations package. In the end, the administration agreed to terminate the NBS and transfer most of its functions to the United States Geological Survey (USGS).[11] The omnibus appropriations bill included restrictions on USGS activities related to biological research. It specified that none of the appropriations to the USGS could be used for surveys on private property without written permission of private landowners. It also prohibited the expenditure of funds for any volunteer program in which volunteers were not properly trained or in which data gathered by volunteers was not carefully verified. The law mandated that the USGS issue guidelines for resource research by April 1, 1996, ensuring that scientific and technical peer review be employed as fully as possible. The bill was signed into law April 26, 1996.

The NBS was formally terminated as an independent bureau on September 30, 1996. The order transferred the bulk of NBS authority and employees to the USGS and renamed the NBS the Biological Resources Division (BRD). The budget of the NBS was cut from $170 million to $140 million. Of the $30 million in cuts, $12 million was cut because of the transfer of some functions back to the Fish and Wildlife Service. The remaining cuts forced the BRD to close a data center in Colorado and a fish research laboratory in upstate New York. Both projects were located in the districts of NBS opponents.

Secretary Babbitt suggested to subordinates at the time of the agency's termination that the transfer to the USGS might actually benefit its core programs. Rather than subject the NBS programs to continued congressional scrutiny and opposition, transferring them to the USGS would "hide them" by placing them in the larger and more established USGS bureaucracy.[12] Since the transfer to the USGS, the BRD's budget has grown from the $140 million it started with in FY 1997. It received $145 million in FY 1998, $162 million in FY 1999, $160 million in FY 2000, and $180 million in FY 2001.

Disadvantages and Advantages of Executive Creation

What the president gained in discretion, he sacrificed in durability. If the NBS had been created by statute, a statute would have been required to terminate it, a statute not likely to have been allowed in an appropriations bill. This would have given the president and the NBS's supporters in the minority a better chance to protect the agency. Of course, the termination of the NBS was caused by party turnover in Congress. Had the Democrats continued in power, the NBS would likely still be an independent bureau in the Interior Department.

The example of the NBS illustrates two important points. First, Congress does not perfectly delegate its authority. Secretary Babbitt used delegated authority from a reorganization plan in 1950 to justify creation of the NBS. Second, the president's creation of the NBS by administrative action resulted in the creation of an agency that was significantly different from what Congress might have produced. Had the president waited for legislation, the NBS might never have been created. A significant portion of both the House and the Senate opposed its creation. Even the measure that passed the House was significantly different from the NBS created by the administration.

DOES CONGRESS DICTATE THE CREATION OF EXECUTIVE AGENCIES? THE AGGREGATE EVIDENCE

There are other cases where presidents used delegated authority in ways inconsistent with preferences in Congress. Presidents created the Peace Corps and the Loyalty Review Board in ways inconsistent with preferences in Congress. A few case examples, however, do not prove a general rule. One way to address this question in a more general way is to analyze the number of agencies created by administrative action over time. Figure 4.1 graphs the number of agencies created by executive action between 1946 and 1997. Substantial variability exists from year to year and from Congress to Congress. The largest numbers of executive-created agencies are created during periods of crisis, such as war or depression. Congress delegates more authority to the president during wartime and during periods of economic crisis. For example, President Truman created the Office of Defense Mobilization and the National Production Authority for the Korean War. The 1950–53 period has the highest number of agencies created. Similarly, Congress passed the Economic Stabilization Act in 1969, delegating to the president power to control wage and price increases. President Nixon used this authority to create the Cost of Living Council, the Pay Board, and the Price Commission to implement wage and price controls.

The fact that the president creates more agencies during periods of crisis begs the question of why Congress did not create them and respond to the crisis through legislation. Congress is ill equipped to act with the secrecy, cohesiveness, and dispatch necessary to respond to crisis, and it explicitly or implicitly delegates authority to the president instead. As a consequence, the president uses this authority to create administrative agencies that Congress itself could not or would not create. It is important to note that once this authority has been granted, it is not easily rescinded (Howell 2000).

Beyond the increase owing to war and economic crisis, the visual patterns defy easy categorization. Figure 4.2 graphs the number of executive-created agencies disaggregated by type of executive action. There is an increase in executive-created agencies during the Kennedy and Johnson administrations. Some of the more famous include the Peace Corps, what became the Defense Logistics Agency, and the Defense Intelligence Agency. The graphs also show a spike during the Nixon administration. Nixon created the Environmental Protection Agency by reorganization plan in 1970, the Central Security Service, the Office of Consumer Affairs in 1971 by executive order, and the Bureau of Alcohol, Tobacco, and Firearms by departmental order. There is a small increase in the number of executive-created agencies during the late Truman and early Eisenhower administra-

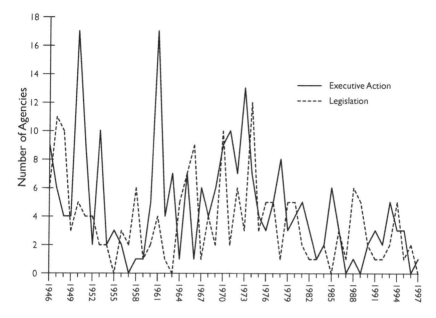

F I G U R E   4 . 1   Agencies Created by Executive Action

tions, a period when party control of the Congress changed and majorities were small.

One of the benefits of quantitative analysis is that it can parse out the different causes of an increase in executive-created agencies over time. If the advantage derived by presidents from unilateral action extends beyond periods of war and economic emergency, this should materialize in the quantitative analysis. If the agencies created by executive action are created uninsulated because that is the way Congress prefers it, then the number of executive-created agencies should be uncorrelated with majority strength. If, on the other hand, majority strength is negatively correlated with the number of agencies created by executive action year-to-year, this suggests that presidents can use the congressional disability to create uninsulated agencies. This could happen in two ways. First, Congress's disability could necessitate presidential creation of administrative agencies to implement legislation Congress itself has enacted. Second, presidents could create agencies and Congress's disability prevents them from responding. In either case, Congress's disability allows the president to create by administrative action an uninsulated agency that either would not have been created by

FIGURE 4.2 Number of Agencies Created by Executive Action, 1946–97

Total by Executive Action

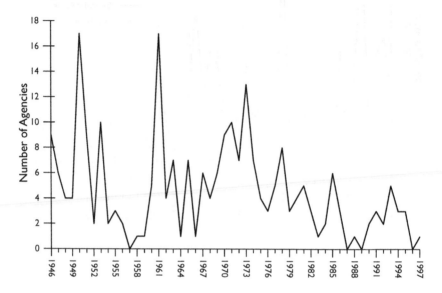

Departmental Orders

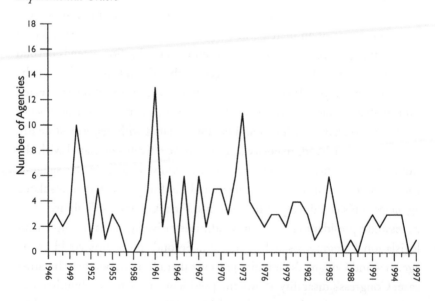

Executive Orders

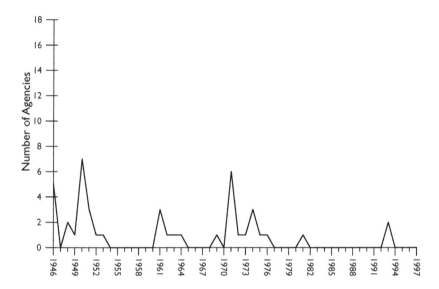

Reorganization Plans

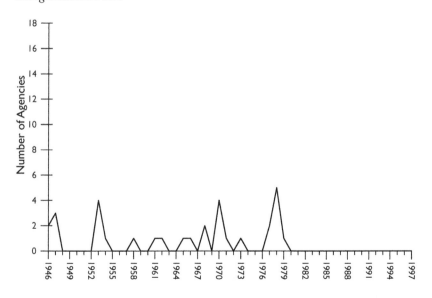

legislation or, if created, would have been created much differently than the administrative version.

Table 4.1 includes the maximum likelihood estimates of a negative binomial regression where the count of the number of executive-created agencies per year is the dependent variable. The number created per year varies from 0 to 18, with a mean value of 4.6 and a standard deviation of 3.9. I employ a negative binomial regression since the data are a nonnegative count and the data are overdispersed.[13] Since there is often a lag of as much as three years between the time an agency is created and the time it appears in the *United States Government Manual*, the analysis includes only count data from 1946 through 1995.[14]

The models include controls for war, yearly unemployment, Democratic president, and divided government.[15] More agencies should be created by executive action during periods of war and economic crisis (as measured by unemployment). I include an indicator for a Democratic president to control for ideological differences among presidents about the proper size of government. All else equal, Democratic presidents should create more agencies than Republican presidents do. I include an indicator for divided government since majorities in Congress are likely to keep a tighter reign on presidential unilateral activity during periods of divided government.

I measure the strength of the majority, or its ability to create agencies by legislation, by the size of the majority in the House. The mean percentage controlled by the majority is 59 percent, and the standard deviation is 4.5 percent. I have also estimated models using size of the majority in the Senate, the size of the smaller majority in the House or the Senate, and the number of public laws enacted per year as measures of congressional strength. The results are the same. If agencies are created by executive action only when Congress prefers them to be uninsulated, then the coefficient on the size of the majority should be zero and insignificant.[16] If, however, the coefficient is negative and significant, this implies that during periods when the majority is weak more agencies are created by executive action.

The final independent variable in the models is average yearly presidential approval. Controlling for divided government, the size of the majority in Congress, and other factors, popular presidents should be able to create more agencies by administrative action. If presidents can use their public esteem to create uninsulated agencies, this implies that Congress does not perfectly control the creation of these agencies. The only alternative is that Congress prefers strong presidents to create more agencies by administrative action. There is no theoretical reason to believe this, however.

The models are estimated with only fifty cases, so the standard errors of the model will generally be larger than if there were more observations. Still, even with these limitations, the models perform well. With the exception of the model of reorganization plans, we can reject the null hypothesis that the models do not improve on a constant-only model (p < .05). The model of reorganization plans is estimated on only thirty-eight cases, since no presidents had reorganization authority after the Supreme Court's 1983 decision in *INS v. Chadha*. The ruling outlawed the legislative veto, an integral component of reorganization authority. Overall, the models of executive orders and departmental orders fit the data well. Importantly, the model estimated on all types of executive action together performs well.

As expected, the results show that during periods of international conflict or economic crisis, presidents create more agencies by administrative action. All else equal, presidents create four more agencies per year during war. An increase in yearly average unemployment by one standard deviation increases the predicted number of administrative agencies by two. Congress delegates more authority to the president during such periods explicitly through legislation or implicitly by not objecting to unilateral presidential action. This confirms the added influence presidents gain through their formal powers in foreign affairs and because of their unique ability to act quickly, decisively, and with dispatch during periods of crisis. Congress's inability to act in such circumstances leads to the creation of more agencies by executive action and consequently less insulation from presidential control.

Not surprisingly, Democratic presidents create more agencies. The coefficients on the Democratic president indicator are significant and positive for executive orders, departmental orders, and total executive action. The ideological preference of Democratic presidents for larger government leads to more administrative agencies by executive action, almost three per year. Although the ideology of the president was a significant cause of agency creation by executive action, divided government was not.

Most important, however, is the sign, size, and significance of the coefficient on size of the House majority. As the majority in the House gets larger,

TABLE 4.1
ML Estimates of Negative Binomial Regression of the Number of Executive-Created Administrative Agencies, 1946–95

Variable	Executive Orders	Departmental Orders	Reorganization Plans	Total
Size of House majority	−11.90*	−3.94*	−1.49	−4.27**
	(7.47)	(2.75)	(8.07)	(2.54)
Presidential approval	0.002	0.014**	0.019	0.009
	(0.020)	(0.008)	(0.025)	(0.008)
Controls, ancillary parameter	1.73**	1.00**	−0.38	0.89**
War (0,1)	(0.61)	(0.26)	(0.77)	(0.24)
Unemployment	0.61**	0.26**	−0.49*	0.22**
	(0.24)	(0.10)	(0.33)	(0.09)
Democratic president (0,1)	1.44*	0.74**	0.26	0.72**
	(0.94)	(0.39)	(1.01)	(0.35)
Divided government (0,1)	0.35	0.17	−0.42	0.04
	(0.75)	(0.35)	(0.72)	(0.31)
Trend	−0.06**	−0.01	0.05	−0.007
	(0.02)	(0.01)	(0.04)	(0.011)
After *INS v. Chadha* (0,1)	—	—	—	−0.55*
				(0.35)
Constant	2.88	0.72	1.36	1.88*
	(3.51)	(1.47)	(4.11)	(1.36)
α	0.60*	0.14*	0.93*	0.15**
	(0.43)	(0.09)	(0.63)	(0.08)
Number of cases	50	50	38	50
χ^2 (7,8 df)	19.64**	15.48**	5.48	25.57**
LR test of $\alpha = 0$ (1 df)	4.40**	4.63**	5.63**	9.44**

NOTE: * Significant at the .10 level, ** significant at the .05 level in one-tailed test of significance. Decimals rounded down to hundredths unless otherwise specified.

the number of agencies created by administrative action decreases. In other words, there are fewer executive-created agencies during the years when the majority is strong. This can mean one of two things. First, it can mean that during periods when the majority in Congress is weak, members are unable to create the agencies necessary for the implementation of laws they have enacted and the president must do it. Second, it could mean that the president is creating agencies at his own initiative and Congress cannot respond. In either case, Congress's weakness leads to more agencies being created by the president, more agencies that are amenable to presidential direction. Increasing the size of the majority by one standard deviation leads to about one more agency per year, or four per presidential administration.

An increase in presidential strength can also marginally increase the number of executive-created agencies. In all four specifications the coefficient on yearly approval rating is positive, indicating that during years with high average public approval, there are more agencies created by administrative action, even when controlling for presidential ideology and divided government. The coefficient is significant at the .05 level in the model of departmental orders and marginally significant (p < .13) in the model of all executive actions. These results, though not conclusive because of the small sample size, at least suggest that strong presidents are able to create more agencies by administrative action than weak presidents even when controlling for divided government.

PRESIDENTIAL INFLUENCE AND
EXECUTIVE-CREATED AGENCIES

Ron Pulliam, the National Biological Service's first director and a scientist by training, expressed surprise at how much politics was infused in decisions about the NBS's creation, its budget, and its termination as an independent bureau in the Interior Department (Pulliam 1995). From the way Republican partisans perceived the agency and its mission to the decisions about which NBS facilities would be closed, the agency was birthed, reared, and ultimately struck down in an environment pervaded by interbranch wrangling and partisan division.

If President Clinton had not requested that Secretary Babbitt create the agency by executive action, it probably would not have been created at all. Republicans and a few conservative Democrats expressed concerns about its activities, and a number of interest groups made a concerted effort to stir up opposition to its creation. As such, no legislation authorizing its creation was likely to pass. The NBS case illustrates how presidents can act unilaterally in cases where Congress will not or cannot act to create agencies.

Had the support for the NBS been larger in Congress, legislation might have been forthcoming. Even then, however, the eventual bill likely would have reflected the interests of the minority. There may have been specific provisions protecting the rights of private property owners or mandated representation of their interests in a commission or advisory structure. As it stood, the NBS, both in the form proposed in legislation and in the form described in Departmental Order 3173, was a standard executive-controlled bureau. Like other executive-created agencies, the NBS was created in a form that maximized presidential control.

One aspect of the NBS story to note is that Congress was well informed about what the administration was doing. Members were involved with the agency, negotiations over the budget, and policies. In many ways the creation of agencies by executive action is subject to the same types of power struggles that take place in Congress. As the NBS case shows, however, the president does have an advantage when agencies are designed by executive action. Opponents are in a weaker bargaining position than they would be if the agency was being created by statute.

Ultimately, the NBS did succumb to its political opponents. The lack of statutory creation ultimately made it easier for the new Republican majority to target the agency. Electoral turnover is a fact of life in public administration, and one of the reasons managing public organizations is different from managing private organizations. It is the fear of just this type of turnover that leads political actors to seek to remove agencies they support from political influence.

Testing the Role of Presidents: Presidential Administrative and Legislative Influence

> The accountability of a Cabinet Department head is not complete
> without the legal authority to meet the legal responsibilities for
> which that person is accountable.
> —President Bill Clinton, October 5, 1999

One of the most dramatic political events of 1999 was the arrest of scientist Wen Ho Lee. Lee, a Los Alamos National Laboratory scientist, was charged with the transfer of sensitive material to the Chinese government. Lee's arrest came on the heels of a widely publicized congressional committee report on Chinese espionage in January and just prior to a report on security lapses at the Department of Energy in June. One response to these security concerns was a proposal in Congress to create a new nuclear security agency to run the nation's weapons labs. The creation and design of this agency was the subject of bitter wrangling between the administration and congressional Republicans. President Clinton and the secretary of energy, Bill Richardson, strongly opposed congressional attempts to create this new agency and insulate it from secretarial control. Congressional Republicans, however, did not trust the administration to make the changes necessary to remedy what they perceived as persistent security lapses in the Energy Department.

The debate over this agency illustrates how preferences over agency design differ in the two branches. The president and his energy secretary, held accountable for the performance of the department and its labs, opposed limitations on their ability to control and coordinate them. Congressional

Republicans, persuaded that the administration was unwilling or unable to resolve the problems, supported removing these programs from their control. The struggle over the creation of this agency also illustrates the strengths and weaknesses of the institutional actors. Each side pulled out its arsenal of tools. The administration threatened vetoes, attempted to preempt congressional action with a milder administrative solution, and used its ability to act first creatively. The majority used omnibus legislation, oversight committees, and large visible hearings to force change.

Hundreds of similar struggles over agency design populate our nation's history. In this chapter I use both the individual struggle over this new nuclear security agency and quantitative analysis of the population of new agencies created since 1946 to demonstrate the influence of presidents in the agency design process. I first present an in-depth case study of the National Nuclear Security Agency (NNSA) that began operations in March 2000. I then revisit the quantitative analysis of Chapter 2 with a fuller data set of agencies and a new focus. I supplement the data set with all the agencies created by executive action and focus the analysis on the role of the president in the agency design process.

PRESIDENTIAL INFLUENCE AND AGENCY DESIGN: THE CASE OF THE NNSA

In 1999 the Department of Energy had a history of security lapses that stretched back to its predecessor agencies, the Atomic Energy Commission and the Energy Research and Development Administration (U.S. House 1999). Since its creation in 1977, the General Accounting Office, congressional committees, intelligence officials, independent commissions, private consultants, and its own inspector general had criticized the Department of Energy (DOE) for security vulnerabilities in six areas.[1] The DOE's long-term planning and management, physical security of nuclear weapons facilities, screening and monitoring of personnel, monitoring of classified information and materials, tracking of nuclear materials, and handling of foreign visitors received the most criticism.

Despite persistent criticism, the DOE had been unable to sustain reforms aimed at improving its security and counterintelligence programs. Although significant departmental change was attempted every two to three years, the fragmented structure of the DOE and the limited duration of political appointees undercut reform attempts. One report claimed:

> Management and security problems have recurred so frequently that they have resulted in nonstop reform initiatives, external reviews, and changes in policy direction. . . . The constant managerial turnover over the years has generated nearly continuous structural reorganizations and repeated security policy reversals. Over the last dozen years, DOE has averaged some kind of major departmental shake-up every two to three years. During that time, security and counterintelligence responsibilities have been "punted" from one office to the next. (President's Foreign Intelligence Advisory Board 1999, 11)

The Clinton administration was no exception.[2]

The Clinton Administration Confronts the Security Problem

In 1995 administration officials intercepted a document from the People's Republic of China describing various U.S. nuclear warheads. Several investigations followed to determine how the Chinese had obtained this information. In July 1997, top administration officials briefed the National Security Advisor on what they perceived to be serious security deficiencies at the weapons labs. The National Security Advisor then requested both an independent CIA analysis and a report by the National Counterintelligence Policy Board on the impact of leaked U.S. nuclear information on China's nuclear capability.

These reports and recommendations led to the eventual issuance in February 1998 of Presidential Decision Directive No. 61. The directive ordered the secretary of energy to make organizational changes within the Department of Energy to enhance counterintelligence activities. It mandated the creation of a new Office of Counterintelligence (OCI) within the DOE, headed by a senior executive from the Federal Bureau of Investigation. The new director of the OCI was directed to prepare a report for the secretary of energy within ninety days of his arrival. His report was to include "a strategic plan for achieving long-term goals, and recommendations on whether and to what extent other organizational changes" were necessary to strengthen counterintelligence activities. It also mandated that the secretary himself report back to the National Security Advisor on implementation plans for improving national security.

On July 1, 1998, the director of the OCI transmitted his report to the secretary of energy, Federico Peña. Peña resigned the next day. Bill Richardson was sworn in as the new secretary of energy on August 18, 1998. On November 13 he submitted his action plan to the White House. It detailed thirty-one changes to be made to the department's counterintelligence programs. They included measures to improve espionage awareness, computer security, cooperation with other intelligence agencies such as the Central Intelligence Agency and the National Security Agency, and selection and training of counterintelligence personnel.

Richardson took additional steps in the spring of 1999 to alter the counterintelligence bureaucracy within the DOE. Among other measures, he granted the OCI direct control over security functions at all DOE field offices and weapons facilities, streamlining the counterintelligence functions of the agency. On May 9 he announced a new "security czar" to oversee the department's counterintelligence programs. Richardson complained publicly about the complex organizational structure, unclear lines of control, and lack of accountability prior to his becoming secretary. His reforms were intended to increase central control, increase accountability, and disrupt the relationships of lower lab employees with allies on Capitol Hill.

Congress Proposes a Remedy

Concurrent with the administration's attempts to remedy the security problems at the labs was increased public and congressional awareness of those problems. The Select Committee on United States National Security and Military Commercial Concerns with the People's Republic of China released a report on the extent of Chinese espionage in January 1999. In March 1999 Wen Ho Lee, a previously anonymous Los Alamos scientist, was fired and subsequently arrested by the FBI for his alleged transfer of sensitive material to the Chinese government (McCutcheon 1999a).

In May 1999 the assistant secretary of energy for defense programs, Victor Reis, went to Congress with a proposal for organizational reform. He proposed a new "semi-autonomous" agency within the Department of Energy similar to the Defense Advanced Research Projects Agency of which he had been director. He made this proposal to Senator Pete Domenici (R-N.Mex.) and Representative Mac Thornberry (R-Tex.) on the same day. He had pushed the idea of a semiautonomous nuclear security agency within the DOE but had been rebuffed. Reis was subsequently fired by Richardson.

Intrigued by the idea and cognizant of the recommendations forthcoming in a report by the President's Foreign Intelligence Advisory Board, the Republican majority in both the House and the Senate produced bills. The Senate version created a new "semi-autonomous" Agency for Nuclear Stewardship inside the Department of Energy. The House bill created a new independent Nuclear Security Agency. Secretary of Energy Bill Richardson strongly opposed the creation of any new agency insulated from his control, particularly a new independent agency, and threatened a White House veto if Congress passed either bill ("GOP proposal" 1999; McCutcheon 1999a, 1393; 1999b, 1475–76; Freedberg 1999). Richardson claimed that the creation of such an agency would duplicate existing DOE functions, blur lines of responsibility, and endanger enforcement of the department's existing health, safety, and environmental regulations. Besides, Richardson argued, he had begun instituting internal reforms and reorganizations as early as February to remedy the security lapses.

Congressional reforms had been proposed before, but the combination of the espionage revelations and the Lee arrest made opposition to DOE reform difficult for members of either party. In late May, Senate Democrats succeeded in blocking a Republican attempt to create a new nuclear security agency through amendment to the Defense Authorization Bill for 2000. The Democrats in the Senate, led by Jeff Bingaman (D-N.Mex.), fought against the bill. They went so far as to threaten a filibuster of the proposal. Bingaman stated his support for reform but suggested "that does not mean we should legislate something that does more harm than good" ("GOP proposal" 1999). He proposed further hearings and study. The amendment's sponsors, Pete V. Domenici (R-N.Mex.), Jon Kyl (R-Ariz.), and Frank Murkowski (R-Alaska), agreed to pull the bill. Domenici suggested, "The Democrats would not let us proceed to debate or vote on this. That's their procedural prerogative, but the point is that sooner or later the DOE has to be restructured as it pertains to managing the nuclear weapons part of America's future."

In June 1999 the President's Foreign Intelligence Advisory Board (PFIAB) issued a scathing report entitled "Science at Its Best and Security at Its Worst."[3] The members of the panel concluded that the DOE's secu-

rity lapses were the worst they had ever seen. The report decried the bureaucracy's past disregard for security reform. The panel placed part of the
blame on the department's unwieldy, diffuse, and confusing organizational
structure and part on the "department's ingrained behavior and values."

The report argued that the only solution to the DOE's security problems was to remove the agency's nuclear weapons functions from normal
Department of Energy hierarchy. The board's report was silent with regard
to many characteristics of the new agency they recommended creating, but
it was adamant that the new agency be insulated from the existing hierarchy. Although the board applauded Secretary Richardson's actions, it concluded that they would be insufficient to improve security.[4]

The board proposed either the creation of a completely new independent agency, like NASA, to oversee the weapons labs or the creation of an
autonomous agency inside the Department of Energy to do the same. The
recommendation was that "the agency would be entirely separated from the
DOE, except in the semi-autonomous case, where the agency director—as
DOE Under Secretary—would report directly to the Secretary. . . . The
agency would have no other bureaucratic ties to DOE, other than R&D
contracting, which would be managed by the Deputy Director" (President's
Foreign Intelligence Advisory Board 1999). The new agency was to be insulated from DOE local and regional offices and existing DOE staffing
and support functions. The board recommended that it have its own inspector general, general counsel, human resources staff, comptroller, and
line in the budget. They recommended that the new agency be created by
statute to "ensure its long-term success" and that the director be appointed
by the president and confirmed by the Senate. The board also suggested
that the director serve for a fixed five-year term and that the director and
senior subordinates have background experience in national security and
public management. The report also recommended that Congress severely
circumscribe the number of political appointees, thereby stemming the "'revolving door' and management expertise problems at DOE."

After the release of the PFIAB report, opposition was more difficult.
Domenici said, "This report makes it inevitable. . . . I don't see how this
can be resisted in Congress" (McCutcheon 1999b). Support began to coalesce around the idea of a semiautonomous agency inside the DOE. Representative William M. "Mac" Thornberry introduced legislation similar to

the Senate version in the House (H.R. 2032). Proponents hoped to attach the measure to the 2000 Intelligence Authorization Bill. Richardson issued a statement rejecting the PFIAB's recommendations, arguing that he did not want to create "a new fiefdom" within the department and countered the legislative proposals with the announcement that retired Air Force General Eugene Habiger would be the DOE's first security czar (McCutcheon 1999b). He also announced that he had asked Congress for $100 million to make security improvements and the implementation of a two-day "security immersion" program for all employees at the nation's weapons labs (Pincus and Loeb 1999). The White House was noticeably silent following the report's release, refusing to back the energy secretary's veto threat.

Republican senators, while applauding Richardson's choice, argued that a stronger legislative solution was necessary. They continued with plans to create the new agency and proceeded with plans to reassign sixty FBI agents to DOE field offices, boost funding for counterintelligence programs, and pass legislation to control high-technology exports (McCutcheon 1999b). On June 22, PFIAB chairman Warren Rudman presented the board's report to a rare joint hearing of four Senate committees. At the hearing, Richardson asked the senators to delay action and to modify their proposal to allow him more direct control over security operations (Pine 1999). The senators rejected Richardson's proposals and pledged to move forward with their consideration of the legislation, altering them to accommodate some of the PFIAB's recommendations.

President Clinton's first public response to the PFIAB's report was noncommittal and generally supportive of Richardson. Clinton suggested that Richardson was "doing a good job on trying to implement the security measures that are necessary." He suggested that the parties involved "ought to try to get together and work out what the best organizational structure is" (Clinton 1999a). Richardson subsequently repeated his threat to recommend a veto but softened his stance toward the new legislation, pledging to work with Congress. He proposed the creation of a new undersecretary position responsible for all national security work but without the creation of a new insulated agency within the DOE (Freedberg 1999). On July 8, reportedly under pressure from the White House, Richardson publicly accepted the idea of a new agency within the DOE as long as security and counterintelligence functions were department-wide rather than confined to the new agency (Pincus 1999a).

In mid-July a House subcommittee agreed to withhold $1 billion from the Energy Department's budget until Congress reorganized the DOE or created a new independent nuclear security agency (McCutcheon 1999d, 1999e). Representative Ron Packard (R-Calif.), chairman of the subcommittee withholding funds, and Representative Christopher Cox (R-Calif.), chairman of the select committee that issued the report on Chinese espionage, both favored a new independent agency.[5] Packard said he strongly preferred a new agency and stated his intent to "push for a separate, independent agency" (McCutcheon 1999d, 1729). Republican senators publicly expressed concern over the degree of divergence between the bills emerging from the two chambers. House Republicans, whatever the cause, had begun to congeal around a bill creating a fully independent agency (Pincus 1999b).

In order to stave off a worse outcome from the House, Richardson and Senate Democrats relented, and on July 21, by a 96 to 1 vote, the Senate agreed to create an Agency for Nuclear Stewardship within the Energy Department. The provision was attached to the 2000 Intelligence Authorization Bill. As part of negotiations with Republicans, Senator Bingaman won approval by voice vote of three amendments to the act. The amendments granted the secretary the authority to continue to use the department's field offices to conduct business with all the department's agencies (the PFIAB report recommended severing ties between the new agency and the field offices), the responsibility of ensuring that other Energy Department programs continue to benefit from the resources at the weapons labs, and the ability to ensure that the new agency meet all applicable health, environmental, and safety standards. All three amendments decreased the degree of autonomy the new agency would have from Richardson and the rest of the department. Richardson called the Senate's action "a good start" and expressed hope that improvements could be made in the bill during conference (McCutcheon 1999e, 1811).

In early August, conferees on the 2000 Defense Authorization Bill decided that their bill was the place to deal with restructuring the Energy Department. House conferees succeeded in including a much stronger proposal than that passed by the Senate in the 2000 Intelligence Authorization Bill. The measure created a new semiautonomous agency completely insulated from the rest of the DOE except that its administrator, an undersecretary, reported to the secretary. The secretary would have no direct control over the agency's budget, personnel, or administration. All secretarial mandates would have to filter down to the administration through the administrator. No other DOE officials, including the general counsel, the chief financial officer, and Richardson's security czar, would have any authority over the agency. The proposal drew a veto threat from Office of Management and Budget director Jack Lew.

The compromise bill was included in the $289 billion Defense Authorization Bill that included funds for military pay raises, military housing, and a number of military projects important to members. Despite threats that the administration might veto the bill, and after minority attempts to amend or delay the bill failed, the House and Senate both passed the bill by veto-proof margins (113 *STAT* 953).

Not the End of the Story

On October 5, 1999, President Clinton signed the defense bill into law. On signing the law, Clinton stated,

> The most troubling features of the Act involve the reorganization of the
> nuclear defense functions within the Department of Energy. The original
> reorganization plan adopted by the Senate reflected a constructive effort
> to strengthen the effectiveness and security of the activities of the Depart-
> ment of Energy's nuclear weapons laboratories. Unfortunately, the success
> of this effort is jeopardized by changes that emerged from conference,
> which altered the final product. (Clinton 1999b)

Clinton specifically objected to the features of the bill that isolated personnel in the NNSA from outside direction, both by the secretary and by the secretary's subordinates. He suggested that this insulation jeopardized health and safety oversight, duplicated existing efforts in the department, and blurred lines of responsibility. Citing the Hoover Commission, Clinton stated that "the accountability of a Cabinet Department head is not complete without the legal authority to meet the legal responsibilities for which that person is accountable" (Clinton 1999b).

A directive in the signing statement appointing Energy Secretary Richardson as the interim head of the NNSA followed Clinton's complaints about the DOE reorganization provisions in the bill.[6] He directed the secretary "by using his authority, to the extent permissible by law, to assign any Departmental officer or employee to a concurrent office within the NNSA." In other words, Clinton ordered Richardson to have existing DOE personnel serve concurrently in the new NNSA, thereby mitigating the insulating effects of the statute. Clinton further suggested tongue-in-cheek that, given the expansive responsibilities the new NNSA administrator had, selection of an appropriate nominee was a weighty judgment that would take time. He directed Richardson to be interim administrator of the NNSA until further notice. Clinton suggested that selection of a nominee might be quicker if Congress were willing to remedy some of the deficiencies in the legislation. He stated: "Legislative action by the Congress to remedy the deficiencies described above [in the signing statement] and to harmonize the Secretary of Energy's authorities with those of the new Under Secretary that will be in charge of the NNSA will help identify an appropriately qualified nominee" (*CQ Weekly* 1999, 2866). In essence, the president had accomplished through administrative action what Richardson had proposed all along, that the energy secretary have direct control over all nuclear weapons activities!

Congress's response was swift and angry. Members denounced the president's actions. Senator Pete Domenici (R-N.Mex.) decried, "It's an absolute frontal attack to say, 'No matter what Congress said, we're not going to do it'" (Towell 1999a). A Congressional Research Service (CRS) report commissioned by Representative Mac Thornberry (R-Tex.) declared parts of the DOE's plan illegal, specifically those allowing DOE officials to jointly hold positions in the NNSA (Towell 1999b). In a testy hearing on October 19 Richardson asked Congress to make what he called "very modest modifications" to the law (McCutcheon 1999f). Republican senators accused Richardson of flouting the law. Senator Fred Thompson (R-Tenn.) said, "It is as if the president has exercised a line-item veto, signing the overall bill but denying effect to certain provisions. . . . That approach is unconstitutional" (McCutcheon 1999f). The House Armed Services Committee set up a special panel to monitor the DOE's implementation of the new law. Representative Thornberry chaired the panel.

Still, some members, such as Senator Domenici, seemed willing to attempt a legislative remedy consistent with the plan passed by the Senate in the 2000 Intelligence Authorization Bill (McCutcheon 2000a). Because of the end-of-session time crunch, however, no immediate action was attempted. Legislative action would have been difficult anyway, since many pledged resistance as long as the energy secretary continued to run the NNSA. After Domenici's pledge to help with legislative changes, however, Richardson agreed to create a search committee for the new head of the NNSA.

On January 7, the DOE sent its formal NNSA implementation plan to Congress. The DOE press release stated:

> Due to a number of factors cited in the plan such as importance of program continuity, shortness of time for implementation, as well as the scheduled change in executive branch administration next January, the plan calls for certain DOE officers to serve concurrently in some of these support function positions. The field managers at selected field operations offices also will serve concurrently in dual positions. (Department of Energy 2000a)

In other words, the plan would continue the dual hatting suggested by the president, decried by the Republican majority, and claimed to be unconstitutional by the CRS. The report received mixed reactions on the Hill. Senator Bingaman praised the plan, claiming that "Secretary Richardson has taken an ambiguous and problematic law, which could have caused long term damage to Sandia and Los Alamos, and developed a workable solution." Republicans, on the other hand criticized the plan's continued practice of dual hatting (McCutcheon 2000a, 2000b). In February, the House Armed Services Committee issued a formal report (U.S. House 2000a). The report criticized the DOE's implementation plan, claiming it "overemphasizes [Energy Department] control."[7]

On March 1, 2000, the National Nuclear Security Agency began operating. Shortly thereafter Secretary of Energy Bill Richardson announced the nomination of Air Force General John A. Gordon to run the new agency. Richardson also announced that he would continue running the agency until Gordon was confirmed. The former second in command at the CIA won praise from Republican lawmakers, but they were still angered by Richardson's refusal to eliminate "dual hatting" in his implementation plan for the NNSA (McCutcheon 2000e). Richardson's memo to DOE employees on March 1 stated:

All the Department's programs—including the NNSA and the offices over science, environmental management, renewable energy and nuclear power—will continue to work together. The Department's current staff offices will continue to provide business, administrative, financial and other support services to NNSA, as needed. It is important to understand that, while there are significant changes within the management structure of the Department, the day-to-day routine will remain essentially the same. All field offices will continue to have the same authorities that they always had but delegated through different channels. (Department of Energy 2000b)

No fewer than eighteen DOE employees were allowed to hold jobs within the new agency at the same time as their DOE jobs, in apparent violation of Congress's intent and past practice (McCutcheon 2000c, 2000d; U.S. House 2000a). Among those with dual responsibilities was Air Force General Eugene E. Habiger, named the DOE's "security czar" after internal restructuring earlier in the spring, and Edward Curran, the DOE's counterintelligence chief.

Congress created the NNSA in response to complaints over lax DOE security. The solution they enacted called for the creation of a semiautonomous agency within the DOE, separated from the day-to-day operations of the rest of the DOE. To allow the two DOE officials with the most responsibility over security to serve in those capacities in the new agency while continuing their posts in the DOE was an affront to the enacting coalition. Similarly surprising was the continued practice of dual hatting for other DOE officials and the use of the field offices. The PFIAB report had recommended their termination.

Endgames

The Clinton administration delayed making a decision on a new NNSA head but finally sent up the nomination of General John A. Gordon on May 8, 2000. The nomination was not accompanied by the standard background details that accompany such nominations. Members were already peeved at the delay in finding and nominating someone to run the NNSA. Some were seeking new legislation to prohibit dual hatting, create an independent office of security oversight responsible to the NNSA administrator (not the secretary), and tighten security measures. Richardson voiced opposition to these measures and Senator Richard Bryan (D-Nev.) put a hold on Gordon's nomination in response to the proposals. Congress was at an impasse with members sympathetic to the president unwilling to support further attempts to limit his or Richardson's authority in law.

On June 12, however, revelations about yet another scandal involving lost hard drives at Los Alamos National Laboratory undermined Richardson's position. On June 14 the House Armed Services Committee held more hearings, and on June 21 the secretary said that he would support a ban on dual hatting and Bryan lifted his hold on Gordon's nomination. Legislation prohibiting dual hatting passed both chambers in late June, and Gordon was confirmed in July. The first dual-hatted employee was replaced in August and Energy Department officials pledged to end the practice fully in the fall, although they had not done so by mid-October.[8]

The NNSA: A Loss for the President?

The story of the National Nuclear Security Agency illustrates two important points about the politics of agency design. First, it illustrates how where you sit in the process determines your perspective on the design of administrative agencies. It was Republicans in Congress who were the most wary of the administration's response to security issues. They worried that the president's appointees, his budgets, and his administrative actions wouldn't be sufficient. The most strident Republicans, such as Representative Christopher Cox (R-Calif.), favored an independent commission modeled after the Atomic Energy Commission to run the nation's weapons labs. The more moderate the member, the less insulated they demanded the agency be from the secretary of energy.

As expected, President Clinton and his secretary of energy opposed attempts to insulate the new agency from their control. Although probably in favor of more streamlined security and counterintelligence functions, they did not favor attempts to take these programs outside the department or the creation of an insulated agency within the DOE. Citing the Hoover Commission, the president explicitly stated his opposition to Congress's attempt to delegate authority to a subordinate DOE official.

Clinton's supporters in Congress also cited the Hoover Commission and favored more administration control. It was three Democrats—Senators Bingaman and Levin and Representative Spratt (D-N.C.)—who were the administration's biggest supporters, attempting to stave off the most insulating proposals. They were also the members who expressed the most sympathy for President Clinton's signing statement and the DOE implementation plan. Only ten years before, however, in 1988, the Democratic majority in Congress had attempted to remove nuclear weapons programs from the DOE and put them in a new independent agency.

The NNSA story illustrates another important point about the politics of agency design. It shows just how much influence the president has in the agency design process in the modern era. The president was involved from the start, both in the legislative process and administratively. Any attempt to explain the creation of the NNSA excluding the president would mischaracterize the process.

In particular, the NNSA case illustrates the importance of presidential unilateral action and how important it is for the politics of agency creation and design. President Clinton and Secretary Richardson sought to use executive action to preempt Congressional action. They rearranged the DOE bureaucracy, creating a new security czar and streamlining security and counterintelligence operations in an attempt to forestall congressional action. Only a lengthy history of security lapses and three extraordinary public events made the president's actions inadequate. When executive action appeared insufficient, the president and Richardson used the veto threat and support of their partisans in Congress to prevent the passage of the most extreme measures.

After the NNSA's creation, Clinton used his administrative influence to circumvent the most insulating characteristics of the new law. He ordered Richardson to serve as interim NNSA head and his subordinates to fill roles in both the DOE and the NNSA. These moves were quite controversial. The Congressional Research Service called the moves unconstitutional, and a special bipartisan House Armed Service Committee Panel on DOE Reorganization suggested that they flouted the intent of the law. Still, Congress's inability to respond legislatively or through the courts provided the president the outcome he preferred until he was months from leaving office. It was only through unusually bad luck from the administration's perspective that President Clinton and Secretary Richardson had to give in as much as they did. Richardson's public position was undermined on numerous occasions by revelations of security lapses at crucial points in the negotiations. Even with this unlikely string of events, the president clearly influenced the outcome to his benefit.

DOES THE PRESIDENT EXERCISE INFLUENCE IN THE AGENCY DESIGN PROCESS?

Does the NNSA story apply more broadly? To answer this question, I now use the whole agency data set, *both* legislatively created and executively created agencies. I want to determine whether agencies created under presidents in a strong strategic position are less likely to be insulated than those created by weak presidents, and if presidents benefit from widespread agreement in Congress or from congressional disability.

If agencies created under strong presidents are less likely to be insulated, then presidents must have influence in the agency design process. The only two other possibilities are unrealistic. First, it is possible that Congress wants to insulate only when the president is weak. There is neither a theoretical reason to believe this nor any existing literature that makes such a prediction.

Second, it is possible that presidents themselves seek to insulate when they are weak. Presidents, recognizing their weakness, could seek to protect policies they care about from future presidents and the majority in Congress by insulating them from political control. This is more plausible but still inconsistent with what we know both theoretically and empirically. Presidents do not face the same electoral or political pressures to insulate, since their election constituency is different and the costs of insulating are more keenly felt by presidents because of their responsibility to coordinate and manage the burgeoning bureaucracy.

The historical record indicates that presidents consistently oppose insulation because it inhibits their ability to manage the bureaucracy and influence public policy. Every modern president has actively opposed insulation in the executive branch and has attempted to increase presidential control. Modern presidents have sought increased presidential control and bureaucratic manageability in the legislative process, through the proposal of reorganization plans and the issuance of executive and departmental orders.

Finally, the dramatic difference in the amount of insulation in agencies created by executive action testifies to presidential opposition to insulation.

Of course, agencies created by executive or departmental order are harder to insulate. Although new legislation or a refusal of appropriations is required for Congress to terminate such agencies, future presidents or department secretaries can often overturn them with a new order. Still, presidents have been quite successful in insulating advisory commissions from their own interference by creating them as commissions and providing party and ideological balance among their membership (Wolanin 1975).

Agencies created by reorganization plans cannot be terminated or reorganized by future presidents without a new reorganization plan or statute. They are as durable as agencies created by legislation. As such, if presidents wished to insulate agencies, they could initiate them by reorganization plan. The fact is, however, presidents do not create insulated agencies by reorganization plan either. During the 1946–83, period when presidents had reorganization authority, agencies created by reorganization plan were substantially less likely to be insulated than agencies created by legislation. Only 20 percent of agencies created by reorganization plan are governed by a board or commission, compared with 45 percent for agencies created by legislation. Only 10 percent of agencies created by reorganization have fixed terms for political appointees, and only 13 percent have specific qualifications for these political appointees. On the other hand, 25 percent of the legislatively created agencies during this same period have fixed terms, and 39 percent include specific qualifications for political appointees.

In sum, if agencies created under presidents with a lot of political leverage are less insulated than agencies created under weak presidents, this implies that presidents have influence in the agency design process. It is implausible that such a result could be due to a congressional preference for more insulation when the president is weak or to more executive attempts to insulate when presidents are weak. On the contrary, it is more likely that presidents generally oppose insulation but must accept it when they are weak. Presidents are held accountable for passing a legislative program in addition to managing the bureaucracy and performing their other responsibilities. Sometimes this means that weak or ineffective presidents must accept more insulation than they would otherwise prefer.

To test whether agencies created under presidents in a strong position are less likely to be insulated, I estimate a series of models using the same indicators of insulation discussed in Chapter 2: agency location (1–5), independence (0,1), governance by commission (0,1), fixed terms for political appointees (0,1), and specific qualifications for political appointees (0,1). I use the same basic specification I did in Chapter 2 except that I add additional measures of presidential influence. I do not repeat the findings from Chapter 2; I focus the discussion, instead, on presidential influence.

Measuring Presidential Strength

There are a number of ways to measure the strength of the president's position at the time an agency is created, including veto use, preference agreement in Congress, whether presidential action occurs in an area where the president's formal powers are greatest such as foreign affairs, and the level of the president's public esteem. Presidents also use administrative discretion to create agencies through executive action. Agencies created during the tenure of strong presidents, as measured by these indicators, should be less likely to be placed outside the EOP or cabinet than agencies created under weak presidents. They should also be less likely to be governed by commission, made independent, have specific qualifications for appointees, or have appointees who serve for fixed terms.

As described above, the veto is a crucial means of entree into the legislative process. Its use, however, does not translate neatly into statements about presidential influence, since weak presidents actually veto more than strong presidents (Hoff 1991; Rohde and Simon 1985). The president who vetoes admits a failure in Congress and signals that he has lost control of the legislative agenda. Indeed, the modern president with the most vetoes was Gerald Ford, the unelected successor to Richard Nixon. Rather than achieving positive policy change, the president who vetoes is left only negating the actions of Congress. As such, I focus on the extent of preference agreement between the president and Congress, Congress's ability to come to agreement, the president's formal powers in foreign affairs and defense, and his public esteem deriving from his position as a unitary political actor and chief executive.

To account for the president's advantage when Congress cannot come to agreement, I again include a variable that is the percentage of seats in the House of Representatives controlled by the majority.[9] I interact majority size with the divided-government indicator. The principal effect should be negative, indicating that the larger the majority in unified government, the smaller the probability of insulation. The sign on the interaction term, however, should be positive, indicating that the larger the majority in divided government, the larger the probability a new agency will be insulated.

To account for the president's added legislative influence from his formal powers in foreign affairs, I include an indicator variable for whether or not the agency's primary function is foreign affairs or defense. Foreign affairs and defense agencies should be less insulated than domestic agencies. Since 1946, 22 percent of all agencies created have dealt primarily with foreign affairs or defense.

To measure variation in the president's public stature I again employ the president's approval at the time an agency was created (Nelson 1996). As presidential approval ratings increase, the probability that an agency is insulated from the president should decrease. I test whether presidents have more influence with partisans of their own party by interacting approval ratings with the divided-government indicator variable. If the opposing party is the majority in Congress, the public esteem of the president will be less influential. Opposition party members cannot hope to ride the president's coattails in the next election. The coefficient on the interaction term should be positive, indicating that during periods of divided government the public esteem of the president is less influential with Congress.

I account for presidential administrative actions by including indicator variables for agencies created by executive action. Such agencies are less likely to be insulated than those created by Congress. Variables indicating creation by executive order, departmental order, or reorganization plan are included, and the associated coefficients should be negative, indicating that they are less likely to be insulated than agencies created by Congress (the base category). Finally, I include controls for the importance of the agency and the possibility of a trend.

RESULTS

Table 5.1 contains the estimates of the probit models of political insulation. The models perform well. Each model improves significantly on the null model, and the results suggest that agencies created under strong presidents are less likely to be insulated than agencies created under weak presidents. The results will be discussed in conjunction with simulations altering hypothetical values of the different independent variables.[10]

TABLE 5.1

ML Estimates of Probit Models of Insulation in
U.S. Goverment Agencies, 1946–97

Variables	Location	Independence	Commission	Fixed Terms	Specific Qualifications
Presidential legislative influence					
Size of majority	−0.05**	−0.05**	−0.04**	−0.02	−0.07**
	(0.02)	(0.02)	(0.01)	(0.04)	(0.02)
Size of majority * DG	0.06**	0.07**	0.03	0.07*	0.06*
	(0.02)	(0.03)	(0.03)	(0.05)	(0.04)
Foreign affairs/defense	−0.47**	−0.28**	−0.74**	−0.13	−0.21
	(0.18)	(0.20)	(0.24)	(0.22)	(0.25)
Presidential approval	−0.011**	−0.009*	−0.009**	−0.018*	−0.003
	(0.006)	(0.006)	(0.004)	(0.012)	(0.005)
Presidential approval * DG	−0.007	0.018**	0.016*	0.021*	0.012*
	(0.008)	(0.010)	(0.011)	(0.014)	(0.009)
Presidential administrative influence					
Executive order[#]	−1.16**	−0.37*	−0.17	−1.69**	−0.67**
	(0.30)	(0.23)	(0.25)	(0.32)	(0.20)
Departmental order	−0.56**	−1.67**	−1.74**	—	−2.03**
	(0.12)	(0.20)	(0.20)		(0.31)
Reorganization plan	−0.22	−0.05	−0.68**	—	−0.79**
	(0.32)	(0.26)	(0.27)		(0.32)
Controls					
Divided government (0,1)	−4.29**	−4.93**	−2.56	−5.10**	−3.97**
	(1.33)	(1.95)	(1.99)	(2.77)	(2.21)
Line in the budget	−0.17**	0.45**	−0.48**	0.17	−0.67**
	(0.09)	(0.16)	(0.14)	(0.15)	(0.17)
Trend	0.00	−0.01*	−0.02**	0.02**	0.00
	(0.00)	(0.01)	(0.01)	(0.01)	(0.01)
Constant	—	3.10**	3.58**	0.97	4.34**
		(1.20)	(0.74)	(2.26)	(1.19)
Number of cases	420	418	418	418	418
χ^2 (13,11 df)	81.15**	129.00**	166.65**	66.47**	74.42**

NOTE: Cut points omitted from table (−5.21, −3.35, −2.74, 2.03). ** Significant at the .05 level, * significant at the .10 level in one–tailed test of significance. Standard errors are estimated using the robust estimator of variance proposed by Huber (1967) and White (1980, 1982) and adjusted for clustering on year. Dependent variable for model 1 is a five-category ordinal variable of agency location—(1) EOP; (2) cabinet; (3) independent agency; (4) independent commission; (5) government corporation or other. [#] indicates different specification for fixed terms model since executive order and departmental order perfectly predict outcome. Coefficient is for indicator of executive creation.

The model controls demonstrate why they are necessary. Consistent with the results reported in Chapter 2, the coefficient on the divided government indicator variable is negative. It is significant at the .05 or .10 level in half the models. On its face, this seems to suggest that agencies are less likely to be insulated in divided government. As in Chapter 2, however, the impact of divided government on the probability that a new agency is insulated is not so clear. The impact depends upon the size of the majority. The interaction terms are all positive and significant in four out of five cases, and the results indicate that agencies created in divided government are more likely to be insulated provided the majority is large enough. Similarly, the probability of insulation is lower in unified government provided the majority is large enough.

Neither the agency importance indicator nor the trend variable has a consistent impact on the probability of insulation. Although each variable is significant in several models, the sign on the coefficient varies from case to case. It appears that the decision to insulate has less to do with the size of the agency than politics at the time the agency is created.

The coefficients for the variables indicating that an agency was created by executive order, departmental order, or reorganization plan are large, negative, and mostly significant. Relative to agencies created by legislation, agencies created by administrative action are dramatically less likely to be insulated. Agencies created by executive order are 36 percent less likely to be placed outside the cabinet, 13 percent less likely to be independent, 7 percent less likely to be governed by commission, and 22 percent less likely to have specific qualifications attached to political appointees. A similar story can be told for agencies created by departmental orders. They are 46 percent less likely to be governed by a commission and 37 percent less likely to have specific qualifications necessary for political appointees. Of course appointees who serve for fixed terms govern no agencies created by executive order or departmental order. Although agencies created by reorganization plan are somewhat more likely to be insulated than other executive-created agencies, they are still much less likely to be insulated than legislatively created agencies. Agencies created by reorganization plan are 9 percent less likely to be placed outside the cabinet, 26 percent less likely to be governed by commission, and 25 percent less likely to have specific qualifications attached to political appointees. Presidents use reorganization authority to restructure the bureaucracy, creating new agencies from existing functions that are more amenable to presidential direction.

The quantitative analysis confirms what was already clear about agencies created by administrative action: they are less likely to be insulated than other agencies. It is not surprising that agencies created by reorganization plan are more likely to be placed outside the cabinet, made independent, and have fixed terms than other executive-created agencies. Reorganization plans most directly involve Congress of all the executive-created agencies, and the degree of insulation reflects congressional influence.

Presidential Strength

In all the models, agencies created under strong presidents are less likely to be insulated than agencies created under weak presidents. This is true even when models are reestimated using only legislatively created agencies. Strong presidents are more likely to get uninsulated agencies than weak presidents are.

The coefficient on the size of the majority party in the House is negative and significant in all of the models. As the majority party gets bigger in unified government, the probability that a new agency will be insulated decreases. If the president's party is one standard deviation larger than the mean in unified government, the probability that a new agency will be placed outside the cabinet decreases by 7 to 8 percent. The probability that this new agency will have the other insulating characteristics decreases between 4 percent and 10 percent.

In divided government, the effect is the same. In three out of five models, increasing the size of the president's party (a decrease in majority size) significantly decreases the probability of insulation. Increasing the size of the president's party by one standard deviation decreases the probability of insulation 0 to 7 percent. The president's partisans serve an important role in defending the president's prerogatives in Congress.

Agencies dealing primarily with foreign affairs or defense like the State Department or the African Development Foundation are significantly less likely to be insulated than domestic agencies. Foreign affairs agencies are 18 percent less likely to be placed outside the cabinet and 10 percent less likely to be made independent. They are 24 percent less likely to be governed by a commission and between 6 percent and 9 percent less likely to be governed by administrators serving for fixed terms or having specific qualifications attached to their appointment. These results are consistent with the expectation that the president is more likely to get the types of agencies he prefers when he acts in an area where his formal powers are the greatest.

Finally, the coefficient on the president's public approval rating is negative in all the models. It is significant at the .05 level in one model and at the .10 level in three. As expected, presidents with higher public approval are less likely to oversee the creation of administrative agencies insulated from their control. Increasing the president's public approval one standard deviation above the mean in simulations decreased the probability that a new agency would have one of the insulating characteristics by 3 to 9 percent.

As expected, the interaction term of public approval and divided government is positive in four out of the five models. This is consistent with my expectation that public approval would be less influential during periods of divided government. The opposition party should be less swayed by presidential approval than the president's partisans are, since their reelection is less closely tied with the president. In four out of five models, however, the point estimates actually indicate that increasing approval ratings would actually increase the probability of insulation in divided government. It is to this finding that I now turn.

Looking More Closely at the Impact of Presidential Approval in Divided Government

The most perplexing findings in all of the quantitative analyses are the findings that during periods of divided government high presidential approval ratings actually increase the probability of insulation in some specifications both here and in Chapter 2. The performance of the interaction term of public approval and divided government is consistent with our beliefs about the calculations of members of Congress. We know that when preferences diverge, members use the president's approval as a proxy for the probability that the president's party will return to the White House after the next election. If the president's approval is high, members of the majority are more likely to support insulation attempts. In the last two chapters, however, I have argued that the president's public stature and approval are sources of presidential strength. These findings, however, call this claim into question. If high approval leads to more insulation in divided government, either public esteem is not a source of influence or presidents who are strong try to insulate.

Fortunately, it is not necessary to come to either conclusion. The model estimates for the impact of approval rating during divided government turn out to be consistent with both explanations. Public approval is a signal both to members in the majority and to members in the minority. The two coalitions view the president's approval in an opposite manner. Members of the majority oppose the president's programs, appointees, policies, and budgets and fear the reelection of someone from the president's party. As such, as the president's approval and prospects for reelection increase, the more likely they are to insulate. The president's partisans, however, support the president and want him to have influence over new agencies. They are concerned only if the president is likely to lose. As such, as the president's approval and prospects for reelection increase, they are more likely to oppose insulation.

So the president's public standing and chances for reelection shape the *preferences* of the two coalitions for insulated or uninsulated agencies. As I argued in Chapter 1, it is important to look not just at the incentives but also at the *ability* of the members to get the types of structures they prefer. Strong majorities get what they want. As such, when the opposition majority in divided government is strong, increasing approval ratings should lead to a higher probability that a new agency is insulated. As this majority weakens, however, the impact of approval rating should change. As the president's party gains power, approval rating will first have no impact and then have the opposite impact, leading to less rather than more insulation.

This is in fact what we see. Table 5.2 includes models of the five insulating characteristics, each with an interaction term combining the size of the majority party, approval ratings, and divided government. So the model contains complicated three-way interactions. Substantively, they show that as the size of the president's party grows, the impact of approval ratings lessens and then reverses, consistent with expectations.

Figure 5.1 graphs the impact of approval ratings and size of the president's party in the House on the probability that a new agency will have fixed terms for political appointees during periods of divided government. The graph includes three lines. The first line simulates the impact of approval ratings when the majority party is small (55 percent), one standard deviation below the mean majority size. The second line simulates the im-

TABLE 5.2

ML Estimates of Probit Models of Insulation in U.S. Goverment Agencies, 1946–97

Variables	Location	Independence	Commission	Fixed Terms	Specific Qualifications
Main effects					
Size of majority	−0.03	0.04	0.00	0.03	0.02
Foreign affairs/defense	−0.49**	−0.30*	−0.79**	−0.20	−0.24
Presidential approval	−0.01	0.09	0.38	0.05	0.09*
Divided government (0,1)	3.65	3.96	17.69**	21.50**	12.83**
Executive order[#]	−1.16**	−0.36*	−0.17	−1.77**	−0.67**
Departmental order	−0.57**	−1.67**	−1.78**	—	−2.07**
Reorganization plan	−0.24	−0.10	−0.71**	—	−0.84**
Interactions					
Size of majority * DG	−0.07	−0.09	−0.32**	−0.39**	−0.23**
Presidential approval * DG	−0.15*	−0.15	−0.38**	−0.51**	−0.32**
Size of majority * presidential approval	−0.00	−0.002*	−0.00	−0.00	−0.002*
Size of majority * presidential approval * DG	0.003*	0.003	0.006**	0.009**	0.006**
Controls					
Line in the budget	−0.18**	0.44**	0.50**	0.13	−0.69**
Trend	0.00	−0.01*	−0.02**	0.02**	−0.00
Constant	—	2.02	1.13	2.11*	−0.66
Number of cases	420	418	418	418	418
χ^2 (13,11 df)	82.80**	138.40**	181.69**	66.31**	85.98**

NOTE: Cut points omitted from table (−4.23, −2.37, −1.76, −1.05). ** Significant at the .05 level, * significant at the .10 level in one-tailed test of significance. Standard errors are estimated using the robust estimator of variance proposed by Huber (1967) and White (1980, 1982) and adjusted for clustering on year. Dependent variable for model 1 is a five-category ordinal variable of agency location—(1) EOP; (2) cabinet; (3) independent agency; (4) independent commission; (5) government corporation or other. [#] indicates different specification for fixed terms model since executive order and departmental order perfectly predict outcome. Coefficient is for indicator of executive creation.

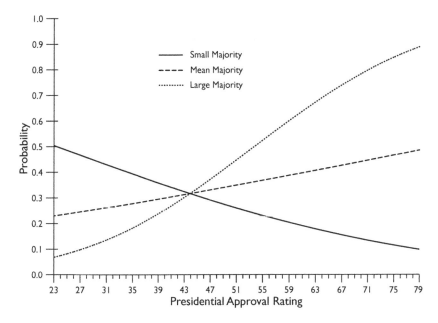

F I G U R E 5 . 1   Impact of Presidential Approval Ratings on the Probability of Fixed Terms During Periods of Divided Government

pact of approval ratings when the majority party is the average size for a period of divided government (59 percent). The final line simulates the impact of approval ratings for when the majority party is large (63 percent), one standard deviation larger than the average majority.

For the two lines where the majority party is average size or larger than average in divided government, increasing approval ratings increases the probability that the new agency will have administrators that serve for fixed terms. Majority members anticipate the return of the president's party to the White House, and they are strong enough to insulate new agencies in response to the president's durability. When the majority is weak, however, the impact of presidential approval changes. Increasing presidential approval actually *decreases* the probability that the administrators of the new agency will serve for fixed terms. When the president's party is large in divided government, its members play a much larger role in the design of administrative agencies, and they view the president's durability entirely differently than majority members do.

FIGURE 5.2 Impact of Presidential Approval Ratings on the Probability of Insulation During Periods of Divided Government

Location Outside Cabinet

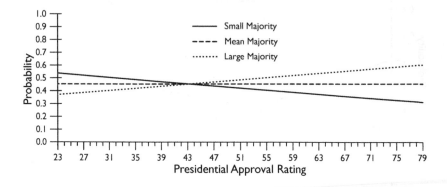

Independence

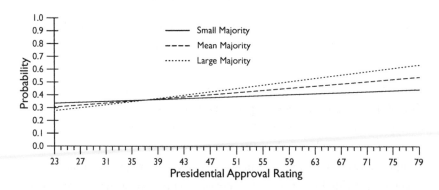

Specific Qualifications for Appointees

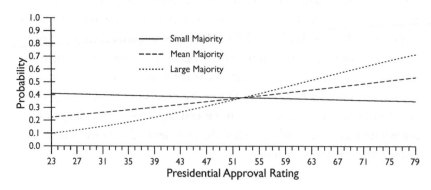

Governance by Commission

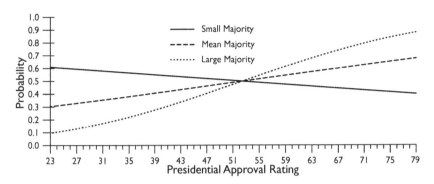

Fixed Terms

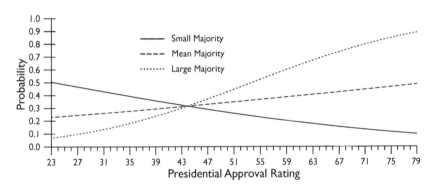

The effect described above is evident for four out of the five models (Figure 5.2). The impact of presidential approval on the probability of insulation varies depending upon the size of the majority party in Congress. Increasing presidential approval decreases the probability that a new agency will be located outside the cabinet, be governed by commission, have fixed terms, or have specific qualifications for appointees if the president's party is large enough.

Disentangling Presidential Influence

The results highlight one of the central difficulties with assigning influence to one branch or another in the legislative process. I argued in Chapter 1, for example, that both the majority and the minority in Congress estimate the likely durability of the president. Their behavior is determined in part by their calculation of the president's durability. In Chapter 3 I argued, however, that the president's public esteem was a source of influence. The arguments being made in Chapters 1 and 3 are actually the same. When looking at Congress, it appears as if individual members are making individual calculations about their preferences and the president's durability, insulated from any presidential "influence." From a presidential perspective, however, influence appears to be exactly what presidents are exercising. Their public standing is changing the behavior of members by making members believe it is in their interest to do what the president prefers.

In the end, the agency design process fundamentally involves legislators and presidents, their interests and their strength. At minimum, the president is part of the agency design process because Congress always considers him when making decisions about whether or not to insulate. More realistically, strong presidents use veto threats, their connections in Congress, their formal powers, and their public esteem to change the behavior of members of Congress so that new agencies are designed to be amenable to presidential direction.

Summary of Findings from This Section

In total, the results provide support for the theory presented in Chapters 1 and 3 in all of its complexity. Importantly, they demonstrate that presidents exercise substantial influence over the design of administrative agencies. Agencies created under strong presidents are less likely to be insulated than agencies created under weak presidents. This result holds for four measures of presidential strength—unilateral action, size of the president's party, action in an area where the president's formal powers are greatest, and presidential public esteem. Although the results are most clearly true for presidents during unified government, they are also true during periods of divided government, provided the president's party is sufficiently large.

GENERALIZING ABOUT PRESIDENTIAL INFLUENCE IN AGENCY DESIGN

One of the interesting aspects of the NNSA case is that President Clinton was asked by reporters about both the appropriateness and the details of the FBI's investigation of Wen Ho Lee and the security lapses themselves. Ultimately, he had to answer for the difficulties. It is no wonder that presidents care about control. If they can be publicly held accountable for the actions of scientists at the nation's weapons labs and field agents in the FBI, their response is likely to be to seek more control. Neither President Clinton nor Secretary Richardson had any love for the existing DOE organizational structure. By all accounts it was a mess. Nor were they responsible for the history of security lapses at these facilities. Yet they had a clear understanding that they needed control over those things for which they were going to be held accountable. This perspective was shaped fundamentally by their view from the executive branch.

In Congress, the concern was for remedying security lapses. Legislators naturally cared less about the control of the Energy Secretary and the president. The objection of the administration to new organizational forms was interpreted in part as obstructionism and half measures, particularly by Republicans. They were less inclined because of partisanship to believe that Richardson or Clinton would or could remedy the security lapses.

The options available to the actors in the two branches ranged from the administrative remedies, including vertical coordination through the security czar, to the statutory creation of a new independent agency. The latter was one of the options in PFIAB's report and found support from key House members. As in most negotiations, the end product of the disagreement between the two branches was something in between. The administration avoided the worst outcome, an independent agency, but it did have to accept a semiautonomous agency inside the DOE. The extraordinary events of 1999 undercut the president and his secretary of energy. If repeated lapses had not kept appearing at key points during the very public deliberations about the issue, and if the president's own advisory board had not issued its very public and scathing report, the administration might have been even more successful.

Still, the president used his full complement of powers. He used veto threats, support from like-minded members of Congress, and unilateral action to influence the outcome. The administration forestalled a meaningful response until it was virtually out of office. Indeed, the reticence of Congress to pursue an even more punitive course after the Energy Department's implementation plan was likely influenced by the upcoming election.

The implementation and start-up of the new NNSA will largely be in the hands of its first head, General John Gordon, but all future presidents will feel the consequences of Congress's actions. Indeed, to the extent that Congress is successful in the NNSA case, it has limited the president's ability to direct the activities and security of the nation's weapons labs. To the extent that Congress removes agencies from presidential control, it is building an administrative state that is less and less amenable to presidential direction over time.

Political Insulation and Policy Durability

Are government organizations immortal?
—Herbert Kaufman, 1976

I have argued from the beginning that political actors seek policy gains that endure. This drive for durable policy gains is an important component of policy making. One of the key ways of ensuring durability is to design administrative agencies to be insulated from presidential influence. However, how durable are insulated agencies? Can political actors terminate or change the structure of insulated administrative agencies easily? If so, their insulation from politics may be illusory, and the policies they implement may be as subject to political interference as any other. The assumption that insulated administrative agencies are more durable than noninsulated agencies has never been tested. If new presidents or majorities in Congress can terminate or fundamentally reshape insulated administrative agencies as easily as their noninsulated counterparts, this has important consequences both for the political actors that choose structure and for the theoretical literature that assumes their value.

To the extent that we understand the causes of agency termination and organizational change, we can determine the effectiveness of insulation attempts. Organizational change usually accompanies policy change (see, e.g., Hult 1987; Szanton 1981). Karen Hult (1987), for example, argues that the creation of the Department of Housing and Urban Development from the existing Housing and Home Finance Agency reflected a change in national housing policy away from a discrete concern for physical development toward urban social problems. President Nixon demonstrated his opposition the Great Society programs of his predecessor by dismantling the Office of Economic Opportunity and parceling out its functions to other administrative agencies (*Congress and the Nation: 1973–1976*, 413–14). Reagan Environmental Protection Agency administrator Anne Burford's administrative termination of the Office of Enforcement reflected a broader policy of reducing enforcement of environmental regulations (Waterman 1989). Recent attempts by Republican members of Congress to restructure the Immigration and Naturalization Service into two agencies are motivated in part by their preference to curtail both legal and illegal immigration through the creation of a new Bureau of Immigration Enforcement (Foerstel 1999). Since organizational change and policy change go hand in hand, an analysis of agency termination can tell us whether policies insulated by administrative structures are durable.

Analyzing the durability of administrative agencies also opens a window of insight into the cumulative impact of past insulation decisions. Agencies insulated from presidential control presumably are not only more immune from the day-to-day pressures of presidents but also more immune to termination than other agencies. If this is true, it has dramatic implications for the president's ability to manage the executive branch, since the president could be managing a population of unresponsive immortals. As such, we need to examine the politics of agency termination more closely and see what impact insulation from presidential control can have on agency durability.

AGENCY MORTALITY

Agency mortality can denote different things. In its most extreme form, agency mortality can mean the complete termination of an agency's formal organization and its functions. In 1995, for example, the newly elected Republican Congress sought to terminate the Selective Service System and all of its functions (Ota 1999). Agency mortality can also mean only the elimination of an agency's separate organizational identity by merger or transfer of its functions to another bureau or department. In such a case the agency ceases to exist as a separate organizational unit, but the functions it performs persist. In 1998, for example, Congress abolished the United States Information Agency and the Arms Control and Disarmament Administration and transferred their responsibilities to the State Department.

How Agencies Are Terminated

Congress can terminate administrative agencies directly through legislation or indirectly by refusing to appropriate funds to an agency. In 1995, for example, Congress enacted the ICC Termination Act of 1995 that abolished the Interstate Commerce Commission. The Office of Comprehensive Employment and Training in the Department of Labor, on the other hand, was terminated after 1982 because of Congress's refusal to authorize appropriations.

Congress also delegates reorganization authority to executive branch actors such as the president or department secretaries. Before the Supreme Court's decision in *INS v. Chadha* (1983), Congress frequently granted the president general power to abolish, reorganize, and transfer agencies by submitting reorganization plans to Congress that were subject to a legislative veto. Since *Chadha*, however, the delegation of reorganization authority cannot contain legislative veto provisions. President Nixon used such authority in 1973 to abolish three independent narcotics law enforcement agencies and combine them into the Drug Enforcement Administration (*Congress and the Nation: 1973–1976*, 566).

The president and his subordinates can also terminate administrative agencies unilaterally through executive or departmental orders if the agencies do not have explicit statutory underpinning. When Congress delegates authority to the president or an agency head to execute a new policy, it implicitly grants the ability to design the administrative apparatus for its implementation. For example, the Agricultural Stabilization and Conservation Service was abolished and its functions transferred to the Farm Service Agency by order of the secretary of agriculture on October 20, 1994.[1] Herbert Kaufman (1976) argues that the dramatic increase in the number of agencies created without statutory underpinning has increased the rate of termination by unilateral executive action.

Why Agencies Are Terminated

Political actors terminate administrative agencies for a number reasons. Principal among them are economy, efficiency, agency failure, and political opposition. Some agencies are trimmed to cut costs. Economy in government administration has historically been one of the principal motivations for agency termination (Arnold 1998). Congressional attempts in the early twentieth century to reorganize the bureaucracy by the appointment of advisory commissions on government management were consistently motivated by attempts to cut costs. This motivation continues to influence political actors. In 1995, for example, Congress eliminated the Office of Technology Assessment, arguing that it was an unnecessary expense in an era of tight budgets. Senator Harry Reid (D-Nev.) explained, "The Office of Technology Assessment is a luxury. It would be nice to have if we had the money we used to have. But we don't have the money we used to have" (*Congressional Quarterly Almanac 1995*, 11–64).

Agencies are also terminated to improve administrative management. Presidents have historically sought a bureaucracy that is both competent *and* responsive (Moe 1985). As chief executive, presidents are held responsible for the functioning of the entire government and have consistently sought to reform the bureaucracy to improve their ability to manage it (Arnold 1998; Emmerich 1971; Moe and Wilson 1994). The presidentially appointed commissions to examine the administration of the executive branch, such as the Brownlow Commission, the two Hoover Commissions, and the Ash Council, have consistently sought to increase presidential control by decreasing the number of independent agencies and impediments to presidential control. President Clinton justified his 1993 proposal to consolidate the banking regulation functions of the Office of the Comptroller of the Currency, the Federal Deposit Insurance Corporation, the Federal Reserve, and the Office of Thrift Supervision by arguing that it would eliminate overlapping jurisdiction, cut unnecessary layers of bureaucracy, and result in savings of close to $200 million dollars (Khademian 1996).

Presidential attempts to facilitate control also occur within departments and agencies. The advent of a new administration usually increases the rate of agency termination (see, e.g., Stanley 1965). Although this restructuring is most evident in agencies inside the Executive Office of the President (EOP), this process also occurs in the cabinet departments and administrations as new political appointees attempt to gain control over the sprawling federal bureaucracy. Restructuring also occurs because new administrations emphasize some programs or policies and downplay others, and these changing policy emphases result in organizational changes. For example, after the election of President Kennedy in 1960, Kennedy appointed Orville Freeman to replace Eisenhower appointee Ezra Taft Benson as secretary of agriculture. Freeman brought with him a commitment to ending rural poverty and coalesced all the existing programs relating to rural poverty into a new Office of Rural Areas Development under a new assistant secretary for rural development and conservation. The removal of rural poverty responsibilities from other administrative units and the creation of the new assistant secretary position meant the complete reshuffling of the Forest Service, Soil Conservation Service, and Farmer Cooperative Service.

Some agencies are terminated because of large visible failures (Carpenter 2000). In the eyes of Congress or the president, agencies may have failed to effectively implement a policy under their charge. As a consequence, Congress and the president choose to reassign responsibility for policy implementation to a new or different administrative agency and close up shop on the old one. The 1989 savings and loan debacle, widely attributed to flaccid oversight and fraud, led to the termination of two administrative agencies. In 1989 Congress abolished the Federal Home Loan Bank Board and the Federal Savings and Loan Insurance Corporation and transferred their duties to a new Office of Thrift Supervision and the existing Federal Deposit Insurance Corporation.

The Politics of Agency Termination

Of course, the termination of agencies ostensibly to improve economy and efficiency or to remedy administrative failure has political overtones. What one party views as a frivolous expense, another party views as an indispensable component of its policy program. Perceptions of success and failure also hinge on political predispositions. The response of partisans in the early 1950s to a well-publicized scandal in the Reconstruction Finance Corporation (RFC) is a good example. Congressional investigations into the lending policies of the RFC in 1950 and 1951 led both parties to conclude there were problems with the agency's lending policy. In particular, both parties were critical of outside influence in the disbursement of loans. Although they agreed on the diagnosis, their remedies differed. Congressional Democrats and the administration primarily pursued reorganization to place the agency under a single administrator and require that all loans be made "in the public interest." Republicans, on the other hand, called the RFC part of a massive "influence racket" under the direction of the Democratic national chairman and concluded that the RFC should be abolished (*Congress and the Nation: 1945–1964*, 1710).

This brings us to the final source of agency termination: political motivations. As Kaufman (1976) argues, those who originally opposed the creation of an agency often succeed in terminating it. Administrative agencies never escape the politics that created them. Coalitions that formed to create a new agency attempt to protect and oversee the new agency over time. The political opponents of a new agency, however, having failed to prevent the agency's creation, try to destroy it if they have the opportunity (Kaufman 1976). History is replete with examples. With the advent of the Eisenhower administration, Secretary of Agriculture Benson terminated the Bureau of Agricultural Economics (BAE) and transferred its functions to the Agricultural Marketing Service and the Agricultural Research Service. The BAE had angered some members of Congress by making unpalatable cotton price predictions, had consistently been opposed by the conservative Farm Bureau Federation, and had angered southern conservatives because of racial overtones in a community survey in Mississippi. President Reagan used his election to propose termination of the Departments of Education and Commerce, opposed by conservatives. The Republican majority justified the termination of the Office of Technology Assessment (OTA) as an effort to trim legislative appropriations. Many Republicans, however, had targeted the OTA because it was a sign of big government and they resented what they believed was its unwarranted expansion into areas such as health care (*Congress and the Nation: 1993–1996*, 895). The Republican House Budget Committee in 1995 listed 372 federal administrative agencies, programs, and authorities for termination (Gugliotta 1995). The agencies targeted by the Republican majority included the Department of Energy, the U.S. Travel and Tourism Administration, the Legal Services Corporation, the Overseas Private Investment Corporation, the National Endowments for the Arts and Humanities, the Federal Maritime Commission, and Amtrak.

WHY SHOULD INSULATED AGENCIES BE MORE DURABLE?

Most scholars believe that administrative agencies are quite durable (Downs 1967; Kaufman 1976; Lowi 1979). As Theodore Lowi (1979, 309) writes,

"Once an agency is established, its resources favor its own survival, and the longer agencies survive, the more likely they are to continue to survive." Other things being equal, the risk of termination decreases. The reasons for this are clear. Younger agencies are less likely to have developed stable relationships with the interest groups, congressional committees, and administration officials necessary for their survival. They must compete with older, established agencies, and they are more likely to make both administrative and political missteps because they lack routinized procedures, patterns of behavior, and strategies that come with experience (Kaufman 1976; Stinchcombe 1965). Over time, political relations stabilize and agencies learn from their initial mistakes, decreasing their risk of termination.

If the likelihood of termination decreases over time for all administrative agencies, the question then becomes whether insulated agencies are proportionally less at risk than other administrative agencies. Does their insulation provide them any additional benefit? The answer is yes. Insulated administrative agencies are more durable than their noninsulated counterparts. The purpose of political insulation is to decrease the impact of changing administrations and changing majorities on the policies implemented by administrative agencies. This same insulation that slows policy change also protects the administrative agencies that implement policy.

Inherent in the delegation of authority from Congress to an administrative agency are efficiency losses known as agency costs. Any time Congress directs an agency to execute a law there will be errors in implementation (efficiency losses) because Congress and the agency have different preferences and because Congress cannot perfectly monitor the agency. Sometimes the difficulties come from simple misunderstanding or miscommunication. Bureaucratic actors just do not know exactly what Congress would do in their situation, and in the process of implementation they deviate from congressional intent. Often it is impossible to discern congressional intent because of disagreements among the members themselves.

In other cases, bureaucratic actors deviate from congressional preferences because they disagree with congressional requests. One of the primary reasons agencies stray from congressional preferences is that presidents use their influence over the budget and their appointment and removal powers to direct agency policy away from the policy preferred by Congress. For Congress, limits on sources of presidential influence reduce deviation from congressional intent owing to presidential interference.[2] In short, when the president has less influence, majority members in Congress are more likely to get the policy outcomes, pork projects, and help with casework they seek.

Agencies located outside the cabinet, for example, are frequently insulated from the annual budget process because they are self-financed. The Federal Reserve Board and the Federal Deposit Insurance Corporation, for example, are funded by assessments to charter banks. Government corporations are also more likely than other government agencies to be funded by sales rather than yearly appropriations. Independent agencies are immune from the pressures and larger policy goals of executive departments that threaten administrative agencies. As argued above, attempts to improve presidential control, cut budgets, and emphasize new programs regularly lead to organizational change and, consequently, to agency termination. Agencies placed outside larger agencies are immune from such pressures.

Diluting the president's appointment powers with fixed terms for political appointees and party-balancing requirements on appointments limits administrative policy change. Removing the president's power to fire diminishes the president's ability to direct agency heads. The most extreme form of such limitations is judicial lifetime tenure. This effectively insulates judges from the most direct form of presidential influence. Congress does not give bureaucratic actors lifetime tenure but has given some appointees tenures of up to fifteen years. Members of the Federal Reserve Board of Governors serve fourteen-year terms, and the head of the General Accounting Office, the comptroller, serves a fifteen-year term. Usually, however, Congress grants administrative actors shorter terms of three to seven years. Although not as insulating as longer terms, shorter terms still serve to insulate administrative actors from presidential direction.

These limitations on the appointment power lead to policy outcomes that are closer to congressional preferences. Congressional involvement in agency decisions is not subject to the counterweight of presidential oversight present in executive department bureaus. The result is that those agencies are more likely to deliver the particularistic projects, benefits, and services necessary for members' reelection efforts. As such, they provide more direct electoral benefits relative to other agencies. Members of Congress are less hesitant to contact an independent agency than an agency in an executive department (Noll 1971), and such agencies are also more responsive to nonstatutory congressional influence (Kirst 1969). Without an adequate presidential counterweight, agencies insulated from presidential control are more likely to produce policy outcomes closer to Congress's ideal point, reducing the risk of termination.

Insulated agencies are also more durable because they are designed to include key interests. Often, in the case of independent regulatory commissions, these key interests are the regulated industries. These interests support and protect these agencies over time. Governance by board or commission, fixed terms for political appointees, and party limitations on appointments are all a means of "stacking the deck." Agencies are designed with these characteristics to ensure that a broad range of interests is represented in agency policy making, usually the interests that have a stake in the outcome (McCubbins, Noll, and Weingast 1987). Stacking the deck with the relevant interests has the additional benefit of ensuring that these same interests support the agency and protect it from termination over time. Deck stacking ensures that the original participants in a legislative bargain have a say in any policy change and can mobilize key members of Congress to prevent termination and policy change (McCubbins and Schwartz 1984). As such, stacking the deck increases the number of veto points in the legislative process.

The Evidence: Data, Variables, and Methods

Unfortunately, very little empirical work exists that tests the durability of administrative agencies, and no research to date tests the relative durability of different types of administrative agencies. No one has tested systematically whether agency hardwiring increases the durability of administrative agencies. The research on agency durability that does exist suggests that agencies may not be as durable as widely believed. Kaufman (1976) and Daniel Carpenter (2000) find nontrivial termination rates for administrative agencies across time.[3] I examined agencies created between 1946 and 1997 and found that over 60 percent of agencies created since 1946 have been terminated (Lewis 2002). If agency structure is as malleable as recent research suggests, this has important implications not only for the literature on insulation but also for presidential management.

I again analyze all agencies created in the United States between 1946 and 1997. Each agency is coded with a termination date (when appropriate) and formatted for event history analysis (see Appendix B). There are 6,550 observations (or spells) on 437 agencies where an observation is a calendar year. So, for example, since the Office of Technology Assessment was created in 1972 and terminated in 1995, there are twenty-three observations in the data set for the OTA. Of the entire sample, 251 of the agencies, or 62 percent, were terminated before December 31, 1997, the last year in the data set. Since we do not observe if or when an agency is terminated after 1997, the data on 38 percent of the agencies is right-censored. Right-censoring is quite frequent in time-dependent data and is accounted for in maximum likelihood estimation (Tuma and Hannan 1984).

The Impact of Insulation

First, I examine the raw probability of survival, comparing insulated agencies versus uninsulated agencies. Figure 6.1 contains a graph of the probability that an agency survives over time, or the survivor function.[4] The survivor function is the probability that an agency survives $t - t_0$ years or

$$S(t|t_0) = \Pr\{T > t|t_0\}$$

where T is a variable indicating the time of agency death and t_0 is the time of birth. The function is decreasing since more agencies live to be twenty-five years old than live to be fifty years old. What we are interested in is the steepness of the decline in the probability of surviving. We want to determine whether agencies subject to more presidential influence have a lower probability of surviving over time. The graph of the probability of survival decreases most sharply for agencies in the EOP and least sharply for independent commissions and other agencies like government corporations. Independent administrations and cabinet agencies have similar survivor functions with agencies outside the cabinet having a slightly lower probability of survival. Overall, the results indicate that insulation from presidential control increases the durability of administrative agencies.[5]

Figure 6.2 graphs the survivor function by these different types of insulating characteristics. All of the insulating characteristics except being governed by a board or commission appear to increase the survival probability of administrative agencies. As agencies age, those without insulating characteristics have a lower probability of surviving. The difference in the sur-

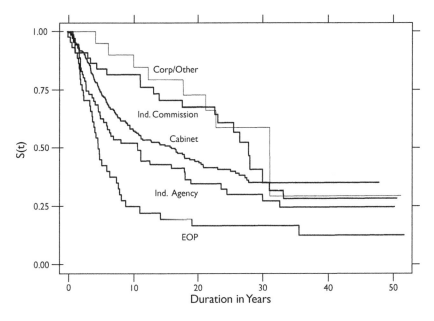

FIGURE 6.1   K-M Estimates of Survivor Function by Location

vivor functions demonstrates that insulated agencies are more durable than their noninsulated counterparts.[6]

Parametric Models of the Hazard Rate

Although analysis of the different survivor functions is an important first cut at the impact of insulation on agency durability, well-constructed parametric models with appropriate controls test the hypotheses more rigorously. One form of such analyses models the hazard rate of agency termination. The hazard rate is defined as

$$h(t \mid t_0) = \lim_{\Delta t \to 0} \frac{\Pr\{dead\ at\ t + \Delta t \mid alive\ at\ t\}}{\Delta t}$$

where t is the age of the agency in years. In other words, the hazard rate is the probability that an agency will be terminated given that it has not been terminated already. As suggested above, the hazard rate—or risk of termination—should decrease over time. I estimate a series of proportional hazards models to test the impact of political insulation on the hazard rate. Proportional hazard models simply test whether the independent variables

FIGURE 6.2 K-M Estimates of Survivor Function by Types of Insulation

Commission Structure

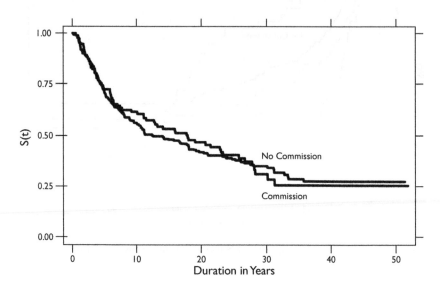

Party Balancing Requirements

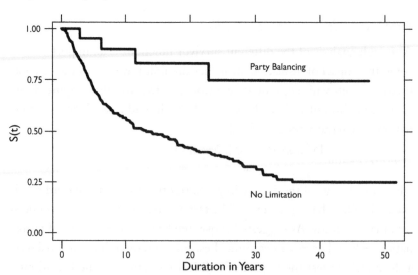

Fixed Terms

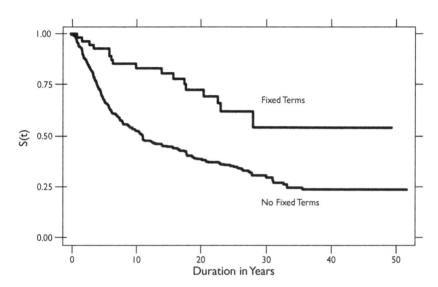

Independent from Existing Agencies

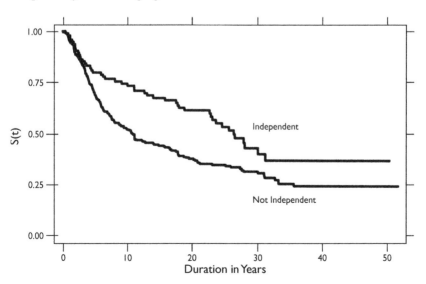

move a baseline hazard rate—which I specify—up or down and estimate by how much. In particular, the hazard rate is modeled as

$$h(t,x) = q(t)\Theta(x)$$

where $\Theta(x)$, a function of a vector of independent variables, simply multiplies some time-varying baseline hazard rate, $q(t)$. We can choose many different functional forms for the baseline hazard rate depending upon our beliefs about what it looks like. Since we believe that the hazard rate is decreasing over time, I adopt a Gompertz specification for $q(t)$.[7]

Independent Variables

The parametric models include variables that account for the motivations for agency termination: economy, efficiency, and political termination where agency failure is considered to be a random process accounted for in the specification of the hazard rate (Carpenter 2000). The models include, first, a variable for unemployment level. Economic hard times pressure political actors to cut spending. One of the prominent means of cost cutting is agency termination and reorganization (Arnold 1998). I measure economic hard times using average civilian unemployment.[8] Unemployment during this period averaged 6 percent and was as low as 3 percent and as high as 10 percent. I also include control for war because Congress historically has granted presidents a great deal of discretion to reorganize the bureaucracy to facilitate the war effort. The variable is an indicator variable coded 1 for the Korean War (1950–53) and the Vietnam War (1965–75).

To account for the agency termination attributable to presidential attempts to improve management capabilities, the models also control for the presence of a new administration, second presidential term, and the number of new agencies created during the year. The presence of a new administration is measured by a dummy variable indicating the first year of a president's term. The indicator variable for second term accounts for the fact that pursuit of reorganization is less dogged in a president's second term (Arnold 1998). Including the number of new administrative agencies created during the year accounts for the agency termination that comes from administrative reshuffling to emphasize different policies.

I also include an independent variable for unified government (0,1), implying that, all else equal, it will be easier to terminate an agency when the president and Congress share the same party. The termination of the Rural Electrification Administration (REA) in 1993 is a good example. Both the Reagan and Bush administrations had sought to terminate the REA but had been rebuffed by Democrats in Congress and their rural supporters. However, when President Clinton assumed office and proposed cutting the agency's budget drastically, Congress and the president negotiated a deal to fold the REA into the Rural Development Administration (*Congress and the Nation: 1993–1996*, 488).

I account for agency termination owing to political opposition by including measures that account for an agency's opponents being in power. I assume for the sake of simplicity that the proponents and opponents of agencies divide neatly along party lines. Of course, this is not always the case. As such, these measures are a tough test of the impact of political opposition. The presence of an unfriendly majority in Congress is measured with an indicator variable accounting for whether or not the party controlling the House of Representatives at the start of an observation is the same party that controlled the House when the agency was created. In 23 percent of the observations (coded 1), an unfriendly majority controlled the House of Representatives. The presence of an unfriendly president is measured with an indicator variable accounting for whether or not the president's party is different than it was when the agency was created. In close to 46 percent of the observations (coded 1) an unfriendly president resided in the White House.

Of course, an agency's risk of termination is greatest when the degree of party change is the most dramatic. An agency created under unified Republican-controlled government, for example, is at its greatest risk when it faces a unified Democrat-controlled Congress and Democratic president. As such, I include an interaction of the indicators for unfriendly majority, unfriendly president, and unified government. The greater the degree of party change, the higher the risk for the administrative agency.

Finally, I control for agency characteristics including whether or not the agency was created by executive action and the size of the agency. The source of agency origin (legislation or executive degree) and the size of an agency can increase the ease or difficulty with which political actors can terminate an agency (Kaufman 1976; Seidman 1998). Agencies created by statute are more difficult to terminate because their termination requires legislative rather than executive action. The collective action problems of Congress make it difficult to secure legislation vis-à-vis executive action. Legislative proposals to terminate an agency must attain majority support and overcome multiple veto points in the legislative process (e.g., committee chair, Rules Committee, filibuster, senatorial hold). Size is measured by an indicator variable for whether or not the agency has a separate line in the budget. Sixty-two percent of the agencies (coded 1) in the sample have a line in the budget. Large agencies are more difficult to terminate (Daniels 1997; Kaufman 1976). If an agency has a large budget, has a multitude of employees, or performs functions affecting many people, it is much less likely to be terminated. On the other hand, a small agency targeted at a specific interest, granted a small budget, and employing few people is easier to terminate.

RESULTS AND DISCUSSION

Table 6.1 contains the maximum likelihood estimates of three Gompertz proportional hazard models.[9] The first model is a control model. The second model includes the five-category ordinal measure of agency location as an independent variable. The final model includes all four of the indicator variables in one model. I do not include the ordinal measure of agency location in this model because it is highly collinear with the different measures of insulated leadership structures.[10]

The interpretation of the coefficients of proportional hazard models can be a bit tricky since the dependent variable is the hazard rate. A coefficient with a positive sign indicates that a one-unit shift in the independent variables *increases* the hazard rate but *decreases* agency durability. So we should expect to see the coefficients on the variables accounting for political insulation to be negative, denoting that they decrease an agency's risk of termination. All the models improve significantly upon the null model ($p < .00$). Importantly, both models accounting for political insulation improve significantly on the control model in likelihood ratio tests of nested models ($p < .00$—1,4 df). In addition, in all of the models the ancillary parameter is negative and significant ($p < .00$), indicating that the hazard rate decreases over time. This is consistent with the expectation that the hazard rate of agency mortality decreases as agencies get older. Older agencies are

TABLE 6.1

ML Estimates of Gompertz Proportional Hazard Models
of Agency Mortality

	(1) Control Model	(2) Agency Location	(3) All Types
Insulation			
Agency location (1–5)	—	−0.25**	—
Independence (0,1)	—	—	−0.58**
Commission structure (0,1)	—	—	0.78**
Fixed terms (0,1)	—	—	−0.67**
Party balancing (0,1)	—	—	−0.99**
Causes of agency mortality			
Unemployment (0,1)	0.06	0.06	0.07
War (0,1)	0.65**	0.61**	0.59**
New administration (0,1)	0.33**	0.32**	0.34**
Second term (0,1)	−0.39**	−0.36*	−0.41**
Unfriendly majority (0,1)	0.19	0.14	−0.02
Unfriendly president (0,1)	0.40**	0.39**	0.41**
Unified government (0,1)	0.53**	0.51**	0.48**
Interaction	0.70**	0.88**	0.97**
Controls, model-specific parameters			
Created by executive (0,1)	0.50**	0.39**	0.45**
Line in the budget (0,1)	−0.21	−0.21*	−0.07
Constant	−4.12**	−3.41**	−4.11**
γ	−0.04**	−0.04**	−0.04**
Number of observations	6478	6478	6418
Number of subjects	423	423	417
Number of deaths	251	251	250
χ^2 Test model v. null (10,11,14)	116.22**	127.62**	147.30**
χ^2 Test model v. control (1,4)	—	11.40**	30.22**

NOTE: Dependent variable: $h(t)$. * Significant at the .10 level, ** significant at the .05 level in two-tailed test of significance.

less likely to be terminated. This provides support for what scholars like Anthony Downs (1967), Kaufman (1976), and Lowi (1979) have believed all along. Administrative agencies become more durable as they get older.[11] In this way, they are not so different from other organizations such as labor unions and firms that have a similar pattern of organizational mortality (Bruderl, Preisendorfer, and Ziegler 1992; Freeman, Carroll, and Hannan 1983; Stinchcombe 1965).

Political Insulation Increases Durability

Consistent with our expectations, the presence of insulating characteristics decreases the hazard rate for administrative agencies. All of the coefficients for variables indicating insulation are significant in the expected direction with the exception of governance by commission structure. I will return to this below. In model 2 the agency location measure is significant at the .05 level, and the sign indicates that the further an agency is from presidential control, the lower the hazard rate. Agencies outside the cabinet have a much lower hazard rate than those located in the cabinet. The hazard rate of independent commissions is close to 44 percent lower than agencies in the cabinet, and the hazard rate of government corporations is 66 percent lower than agencies in the cabinet.[12]

When most scholars think of insulated political structures, they think of independent regulatory commissions. Three important components of these agencies are that they are independent, have leaders that serve for fixed terms, and have party-balancing requirements for presidential appointments. The Federal Election Commission, for example, is independent and has six commissioners—three Democrats and three Republicans—who serve for fixed terms. The coefficients on all three characteristics of independent regulatory commissions are significant at or close to the .05 level in two-tailed tests of significance. Any agency placed outside of existing bureaucratic agencies has a hazard rate that is about 44 percent lower than agencies inside other agencies. Agencies headed by officials who serve for fixed terms have a hazard rate that is 49 percent lower than other agencies. The hazard rate for agencies that have party limitations on appointments is 63 percent lower than other agencies. As expected, party-balancing limitations are the form of deck stacking that has the largest impact on durability. Insulated agencies do appear to entrench a broader scope of interests than other agencies. Deck stacking makes a wider range of people interested in the persistence of an agency, decreasing an agency's risk of termination.

The only exception to the pattern of insulating characteristics increasing agency durability is governance by board or commission. The coefficient on governance by commission is significant, but the sign is the opposite of what was expected. It is possible that commission structures without fixed terms, independence, or party-balancing requirements have a higher hazard rate simply for their lack of efficiency. Although a commission with equal representation, fixed terms, and a measure of autonomy is insulated, a commission whose members can be replaced and appointed at will could simply be poorly managed. Commissions are less responsive to hierarchical direction, and it is more difficult for them to plan, manage, and come to consensus. It is important to note that our previous examination of the survivor functions demonstrated the durability of *independent* commissions. From the agency location model (2) we know that independent commissions are more durable than other agencies. They have a 44 percent lower hazard rate than agencies in the cabinet. This implies that commissions that are not independent have a higher hazard rate. When models were reestimated controlling for presidentially and legislatively created commissions, it was the presidentially created boards and commissions like the Domestic Policy Council that were driving the results. In fact, though not significant, the coefficient on legislatively created commissions was negative, indicating a lower hazard rate.

In total, while the picture for commissions is a bit more complicated than anticipated, the presence of insulating characteristics like independence, fixed terms, and party-balancing limitations on appointments significantly decrease the hazard rate for administrative agencies. In addition, those agencies that are further removed from direct presidential influence have a lower hazard rate. When political actors choose to insulate administrative agencies, they appear to do so for good reasons. Insulated administrative agencies are more durable than other agencies. These results are consistent with recent literature that suggests that political actors choose bureaucratic structures strategically (Horn 1995; McCubbins, Noll, and Weingast 1989; Moe 1989, 1990b).

Causes of Agency Termination

My expectations for the causes of agency mortality were also generally validated by the results. Although one macropolitical cause of agency mortality, namely unemployment, did not significantly increase the hazard rate of agency mortality, the variables representing wartime did significantly increase the hazard rate of agency mortality. Presidentially led organizational change and political opposition also significantly alter the hazard rate. The variable accounting for the advent of a new presidential administration is significant at well below the .05 level in every model and increases the hazard rate of administrative agencies by about 39 percent. This confirms the work of Peri Arnold (1998), who argues that almost all modern presidents have sought to reorganize the bureaucracy soon after their election. The hazard rate of agency mortality decreases in the second term of presidential administrations, suggesting that most presidential attempts to reorganize occur in a president's first term.

Party change significantly increases the hazard rate of agency mortality. However, party change in the White House seems to pose a greater threat to administrative agencies than party change in Congress. The coefficient on the variable indicating an unfriendly president in the White House is significant at well below the .05 level in each model. An unfriendly president in the White House increases the hazard rate by close to 50 percent. New presidents, particularly presidents from the opposite party, can dramatically increase the hazard rate for agencies created under the previous regime.

Unified government also increases the hazard rate of agency termination. The hazard rate of agency mortality is 70 percent higher during periods of unified government than divided government. As expected, the risk to administrative agencies is higher the greater the degree of party change. When an unfriendly majority is in Congress, an unfriendly president is in the White House, and there is unified government, the hazard rate for agencies increases dramatically. The coefficient on the interaction term is significant at well below the .05 level in all the models. Agencies created under unified government of one party but existing under unified government of the other party have a hazard rate that is 240 percent higher than if the party change had never occurred!

Finally, agencies created by executive actors and smaller agencies have higher hazard rates than agencies created by legislation and larger agencies.

The coefficients on the variable accounting for creation by executive action are all significant at well below the conventional .05 level. The hazard rate for agencies created by executive action is 75 percent greater than agencies created by legislation. This suggests that agencies created by statute are insulated just by virtue of their statutory underpinning. Agencies with a line in the budget appear to be more durable than their counterparts. They are about 19 percent less likely to be terminated than agencies that do not have a separate line in the budget.

In sum, through an analysis of the survivor functions of insulated and noninsulated agencies and parametric models of agency durability, it is clear that insulated agencies are substantially more durable than noninsulated agencies. These findings have important implications both for the theory of agency design and for what we know about agency termination. First, the strategic use of insulating structures to increase the durability of policy gains appears to be a well-thought-out strategy. Indeed, agencies placed outside the cabinet are significantly more durable than other agencies. Independent agencies, agencies governed by administrators that serve for fixed terms, or commissions with party-balancing limitations on appointment powers have a lower risk of termination than other agencies. Second, like decisions about design, decisions about termination appear to rest as much on politics as on concerns about costs or efficiency. Those agencies subject to the most extensive party change are the most at risk. They appear never to escape the politics that created them.

AGENCY DURABILITY AND THE EFFECTIVENESS OF INSULATING STRATEGIES

The National Biological Service and the National Nuclear Security Administration suffered two different fates. The NBS was created as an executive branch bureau by executive action, supported by the administration but facing significant opposition in Congress. The NNSA was created as a semiautonomous agency inside the Energy Department by statute, the product of a bargain between the executive and legislative branches. The NNSA will survive, but the NBS did not, the victim of electoral turnover in Congress. This chapter showed that agencies like the NNSA, created by statute and somewhat insulated from political control, are more durable than other agencies. Though new administrations come and assert control, though electoral turnover brings new policy priorities and new risks for agencies, and though times of crisis promote bureaucratic reshuffling, insulated agencies are more durable. The dilution of presidential influence makes such agencies more responsive to Congress in the two branches' struggle for control over bureaucratic policy making.

I began this book with an argument about the importance of separation of powers for understanding agency design, but separation of powers also shapes governance and the decision to terminate agencies. Congress and the president continue to struggle for control over agencies after their creation through budgets, appointments, and agency directives. The initial design decision fundamentally shapes the effectiveness of each branch's overtures.

Agency termination is the ultimate act of political control. The extent to which insulated agencies are less susceptible to termination proves the value of insulation to political actors. Insulation matters. How the two branches view insulation, however, is shaped both by their unique institutional perspectives and by their policy preferences. Presidents oppose insulation attempts precisely because of how it limits their control. The proliferation of insulated agencies has dramatic consequences for presidential management and for the provision of policy outcomes through administrative action. Presidents increasingly are faced with an accumulation of agencies over which they have little control. Removed from presidential control by commission structures, independence, fixed terms, and party-balancing requirements, these agencies are less directly accountable to the president.

What the Politics of Agency Design Tells Us About American Politics

> Today there is not much chance to create a new agency;
> almost every agency one can imagine already has been created.
> —James Q. Wilson, 1989

By the end of 2001, the new Transportation Security Administration (TSA) was beginning operations. The agency was created in response to the September 11, 2001, terrorist attacks and authorized in the Aviation and Transportation Security Act enacted November 19, 2001. Included in the legislation were provisions requiring the agency to provide security at hundreds of airports across the country. The agency is responsible for hiring thirty thousand qualified baggage screeners and implementing a system for screening checked luggage (within sixty days of the bill's passage). The agency must also perform background checks on the close to 750,000 airport employees with access to secure areas at airports. The TSA includes the Air Marshals and has intelligence gathering and disaster-response duties. When it becomes fully operational, it will be larger than the Federal Bureau of Investigation, the Customs Service, and the Border Patrol combined (Peckenpaugh 2002).

The agency was created by statute after only a few weeks of deliberation in response to public pressure for visible action on airline safety. The administration sought more management discretion than provided in the law. In particular, it preferred working with the existing baggage screening operations at the nation's airports rather than taking over these functions directly and requiring that baggage screeners be federal employees. Some observers worried about the management implications of an agency created so hastily with an unclear mission, inadequate funding, and congressionally imposed deadlines (Peckenpaugh 2002).

The administration's earlier request that Congress hold off on legislative action either to create a homeland security agency or to authorize the existing Office of Homeland Security was partly driven by similar concerns to those being expressed about the TSA. The White House feared that such actions would be hasty, ill considered, and ultimately might jeopardize the administration's ability to control the outcome. For Congress the more proximate concern was to create an agency to respond to airline and airport safety concerns quickly and visibly. Even in crisis there are fundamental disagreements between the two branches, both because of unique institutional vantage points and because of partisan differences.

Does Design Really Matter?

Do the different preferences for design really matter? Is one agency design better than another? This question can be answered in two ways. First, it can be answered from the perspective of the political actors involved in the decision. For presidents, the answer is almost always yes. Presidents are institutionally situated to favor those designs that maximize presidential control and influence and limit inefficiencies caused by duplication, overlap, and fragmentation of responsibility. Members of Congress change their opinions depending upon how much they share the president's preferences for policy. Their opinions change depending upon who is likely to propose budgets, nominate appointees, and issue executive decrees both now and in the future.

A second way of answering the design question is to focus on the impact of different designs on the effectiveness of the administrative state as a whole. Which designs will provide the valued outputs with the lowest amount of time, personnel, and other valuable resources? The answer to this question, too, depends upon the preferences of the public at large. Which agency designs will best reflect the interests of the public? Are deviations from the public interest more likely to occur because of presidential political influence over agencies or because of inefficiencies resulting from insulation from democratic control?

My bias is toward the hierarchically structured bureau. It is, of course, impossible to design an administrative state perfectly differentiated into mutually exclusive, functionally organized bureaus. The size and complexity of government action will necessarily require the formation of interagency committees and vertical coordination coming from the highest levels. Still, a bit more presidential influence in agency design will likely provide efficiency gains in the long run. Most political actors who recognize the need for management discretion and have supported study commissions on executive branch organization and granted presidential reorganization authority share my view.

There will be some policy areas where the consequences of policy discontinuities are so great, however, that removing them from direct presidential control will provide long-term benefits. Delegating control over interest rates and monetary policy to the Federal Reserve, for example, is probably a case where the losses of efficiency in coordination are outweighed by the potential policy losses from flip-flopping presidential economic policy. That said, many agencies that are insulated from political control could easily have been created as hierarchically structured bureaus inside the existing cabinet structure without dramatic consequences for the public.

Ultimately, the concern the public should have over agency design is the same one articulated by the framers and ratifiers of the Constitution. How can we energize an effective and responsible administration of the laws while protecting ourselves from the arbitrary use of power? The most effective administration can also be a perfectly abusive one. However, many attempts to remove policies from presidential control are less concerned with the arbitrary use of power than political predilections. In the end, we should choose to insulate agencies from presidential control judiciously.

Agency Design: What Have We Learned?

What the cases of the Transportation Security Administration, the Office of Homeland Security (OHS), and other agencies like the National Biological Service and the National Nuclear Security Agency illustrate is that the design of administrative agencies is fundamentally a political process. Politicians know that agency design decisions have huge consequences for the safety of airline travelers, the protection of domestic security, the provision of unbiased scientific information on biological resources, and the protection of America's nuclear secrets. Administrative agencies make and implement these types of public policies.

With the growth in federal government responsibility and the increasing complexity of public policy, political actors are delegating increasing amounts of authority to executive branch actors. How the executive branch is designed helps determine both the content of the policy and the success of its implementation. At the most basic level it determines who has influence and who does not.

As a consequence, prior to any budget being passed, prior to any appropriation being given, and prior to any nominee assuming control, political actors struggle over the design of administrative agencies. They choose consciously and carefully because of the varied impacts of different designs on public policy. Political actors in Congress and the executive branch struggle mightily over what might seem to be insignificant details of agency design. Congressional partisans from both parties and the president pitched a three-way battle over the creation and design of both the National Biological Service and the National Nuclear Security Administration. They clearly understood the implications of their decisions for Department of Interior research, for the DOE and weapons labs, and for their political careers.

To say that agency design is political is not to say that it is incomprehensible. On the contrary, through an understanding of the incentives of political actors derived from their institutional roles and preferences we can learn a lot. In the famous words of Miles's Law, "Where you stand depends upon where you sit." The institutional position of the president and members of Congress fundamentally determines the parameters within which they make decisions about agency design. Their different constituencies and responsibilities shape how they view agency design. Parochial reelection interests mean that Congress cares less about the long-term manageability of the executive branch and more about short-term visible responses to public problems. The president, held accountable for policy outputs and the performance of the bureaucracy, wants more control rather than less.

Disagreements between the branches arise when there is significant opposition to presidential control in Congress. Legislative preferences for different agency designs are the product of policy preferences and the degree of uncertainty about implementation. A new agency's supporters take into account the likely actions of the president toward the agency. Are they likely to support the president's nominees, budgets, and agenda? If they are not sure, will the majority supporting the agency be strong enough to watch over the agency themselves? Will people who support the agency, either in the White House or in Congress, be able to protect and oversee the new agency over time?

An agency's opponents also take into account the likely actions of the president toward the agency. Will the new president support the agency enthusiastically in his nominees, budgets, and administrative and public actions? Or will the president drag his feet nominating, proposing adequate budgets, and providing the necessary White House support for an agency? The opponents, like the proponents, will have to calculate the likely longevity of the preferences of the current president. Are they likely to support the policies of the next president?

Ultimately, the dynamics of congressional policy making will help determine the shape of the outcome. Bargaining between these groups, loosely defined, will determine the eventual outcome. As in any bargaining environment, the relative strength of each party will help determine the outcome. Strong majorities get what they want. Smaller majorities are more beholden to moderates who are less enthusiastic about the new agency.

Of course, the preferences and influence of the president complicate the dynamics of congressional policy making. Presidents consistently oppose congressional attempts to insulate new administrative agencies from presidential control. President Clinton opposed congressional attempts both to limit the NBS and to insulate the NNSA from secretarial control. Like the supporters of a new agency, however, the president's power and influence varies based upon preferences in Congress, the field in which presidents are acting (foreign or domestic), and their public esteem. Presidents in a strong strategic position are less likely to preside over the creation of insulated agencies than weak presidents are.

The political struggle over agency creation and design does not end after the agency is created. Republican opponents of the National Biological Service sought to terminate the agency in 1995 when they assumed the majority in Congress. The coalition that sought the creation of the new agency tried to protect it over time. The opponents of the new agency, however, upon gaining power, succeeded in eliminating it as an independent agency. The case of the NBS demonstrates that legislative fears about future political influence are real and illustrates how political actors could insulate for understandable reasons.

In his signing statement of the Defense Authorization Act, the act that authorized the NNSA, President Clinton cited the Brownlow Commission report to criticize Congress's design. His citation of this report and his opposition to the insulated design of the NNSA illustrate the important and consistent differences in the way that actors in the two branches view agency design. The relative influence of actors in the two branches over outcomes depends upon their relative bargaining strength.

What is clear is that when Congress exercises more influence in the process, there exists a higher probability that agencies will be insulated from presidential control. This has important consequences for American public administration. Over time, the number of agencies created to be insulated from presidential control accumulates. The bureaucracy becomes less amenable to presidential coordination and management. It includes more duplication, more overlapping responsibilities, and more fragmentation of political control. Rather than place new agencies with related responsibilities within existing hierarchically structured executive departments, agencies are created independent and located outside executive departments. Agencies are created with fewer political appointees. These appointees are more likely to have specific qualifications attached to their nomination and prohibitions against presidential removal. Congress increasingly delegates authority to subordinate officials, giving them independent authority from their nominal superiors.

Presidents, to the extent that they recognize their strategic position in the constitutional system, are the only natural opponents of this trend. Modern presidents have learned quickly. Faced with the consequences of past design choices and aided by advice from the growing institutional presidency, presidents have made choices with their institutional interests in mind. Given the importance of executive branch policy making, we should not express shock when presidents try to fend off insulation attempts, "politicize" appointments, or try to increase the resources of the institutional presidency. Each is crucial in improving presidential control by decreasing preference divergence in the bureaucracy and by improving monitoring.

The Approach

To uncover the logic undergirding the politics of agency design, I used a rational choice approach. This approach comes with advantages and disadvantages. I have simplified in an attempt to explicitly build theory that produces testable implications and have borrowed from existing works in the New Economics of Organization tradition to theorize about what the president wants in the agency design process and when he is likely to get it. I focus on the microlevel decisions of presidents and members of Congress and describe how strategies are shaped by institutional constraints.

By its very nature this approach simplifies, meaning I had to purposefully leave out some aspects of the agency design decision. I focused only on those forms of insulation that remove agencies from presidential control. I did not look at the specificity of statutes, the design of administrative procedures, or other budgetary tools for insulating agencies from political control (see Huber, Shipan, and Pfahler 2001; McCubbins, Noll, and Weingast 1987; and McCubbins and Schwartz 1984). I also simplified the decision-making process of political actors making an agency design decision. I downplayed the extent to which presidents would trade control over new agencies for other policy goals (see McCarty 1999 and McCubbins, Noll, and Weingast 1989). I also did not include concerns that members of Congress have about the durability of their own majority in my analysis. This plays a big role in Moe's (1989) theory of the politics of bureaucratic structure. Finally, I downplayed the different politics associated with different types of government functions and the role that interest groups play, something that plays a large role in Horn's (1995) theory of agency design.

One potential criticism of the theory is that it is too simplistic. Yet every explanation is a simplification of what happens in the real world. It is a matter of degree. By sacrificing this complexity, regularities in agency design were made clear. I could make a number of substantive predictions about agency design that were tested with both qualitative and quantitative

data. The success of the theoretical enterprise can partly be judged by its conformity to reality. The predictions of the theory held up remarkably well in empirical tests.

Looking to the Future

The case of the Transportation Security Agency illustrates the important fact that agency design is a fundamental part of the American political process. Agencies are created and terminated all the time. Understanding this process helps us forecast how the politics of creation will play out in the future. Several implications emerge for the future of agency design in the United States. First, in the immediate future with the war on terror, Congress will be more likely to defer to the president, since the president is strategically the strongest when acting in foreign affairs and Congress has the fewest incentives to take the lead. Presidents have more information and have the ability to act first. They also exercise more control over public opinion. Congress has already been deferential to the president with the creation of the TSA and the creation of the OHS. The TSA is a hierarchically structured subcabinet agency, and the OHS was created by executive action with little congressional input.

We may also see agreement on a reorganization of executive branch agencies with domestic security responsibilities into one hierarchically organized agency, provided the proposal comes from the administration and is sold effectively to Congress. Overcoming opposition from the agencies themselves and their patrons in Congress is always difficult, but offering the agencies significant budget increases could go a long way toward pushing this legislation through. Without presidential support it is unlikely such a measure could pass.

Second, as the war on terror loses its ability to tie congressional and presidential interests together, the divided control of Congress will lead to fierce competition over control of the administrative state. Since the current majorities in Congress are not large, we should expect the president to create more administrative units by executive action rather than legislation. Those agencies created by legislation are more likely to reflect the interests of the president's opponents, since they will have to be consulted to get any statutes enacted. New agencies created by statute will be more likely to be placed outside the cabinet departments and to ensure the representation of minority interests and to have autonomy from presidential direction.

Finally, we should expect the two branches to continue struggling over the design, control, and termination of executive branch agencies. The Constitution, by neither describing nor empowering the administrative state, has left it up to politicians in the two branches to do this job. The bureaucracy is fundamentally and inescapably a political object. In the modern period it has become increasingly important to control the administrative state to secure public policy outputs. With the increasing scope and complexity of the government's business, we should expect to see only more struggle over the design and control of administrative agencies.

APPENDICES

Administrative Agency Insulation Data Set

DATA SOURCES, COLLECTION, AND VARIABLES

This data set consists of a comprehensive sample of U.S. government administrative agencies created between 1946 and 1997.[1] The *United States Government Manual* (*USGM*), a serial published by the Government Printing Office, is the primary source for this data set. Information from the *Congressional Directory* (1946–50), the *Federal Regulatory Directory* (1998), Whitnah (1983), Kurian (1998), and other federal government documents and publications supplements the information from the *USGM*.

Each agency created during this period is one observation. The determination of what constitutes a new agency is not a trivial consideration (Emmerich 1971; Whitnah 1983). Political actors create and terminate agencies frequently, but they rarely terminate the functions these bureaucracies perform. New organizational units often perform functions similar to those of previously existing agencies. In this data set an agency was considered to be a new agency if it had a new name and different functions from any previously existing agencies. So, for example, the National Archives and Records Service (NARS), created in the General Services Administration in 1949, is considered a new agency even though it retained much of the character of the National Archives Establishment, a previously existing independent agency. In addition to a change in location, the NARS had a new name and was given new responsibilities over federal government records. On the other hand, the data set excludes the Social Security Administration (SSA), created as an independent agency in 1994. Although the newly independent SSA adopted some new responsibilities when it became independent, its name did not change.

Bureaucracies vary in size from cabinet departments, major administrations, and bureaus to offices and programs. The data set includes cabinet departments, administrations, bureaus, and large offices. It excludes programs and offices not large enough to be included in the *USGM*. So, for example, the data set includes the Office of Economic Opportunity, a significant part of President Johnson's War on Poverty, but excludes the Learn and Serve America program run through the Corporation for National and Community Service. The data set is subject to the criticism that it includes too many trivial organizational units. However, their inclusion in the *USGM* provides an easy, unbiased decision rule and indicates their importance. The data set also provides budget data for each unit as a rough way of measuring the relative importance of the different organizational units. It also provides an indicator variable that allows for the exclusion of all organizational units that are subsidiary to larger departments, administrations, or commissions.

Collection of the Data

The first step in constructing the data set was determining what agencies to include. This determination proceeded in three stages described below. After I compiled a complete list, I added variables to account for agency origin, the degree of agency insulation, other agency characteristics, political context, and various controls.

Stage One

In the first stage, I compiled a complete list of all bureaucratic agencies created in the federal government between 1946 and 1996. The compilation of agencies proceeded in three sweeps. In the first sweep I paged through fifty years of the *USGM* in five-year intervals and pulled out major bureaucratic agencies. These data were used in a pilot study in 1997. In the second sweep, I added agencies that had been created after 1945 but had been terminated before 1996. Each *USGM* contains an appendix listing all such agencies. In the final sweep, I added all agencies not included in the first two sweeps but still included in the index of the 1996–97 *USGM*. In total, the data set included 776 federal government agencies created between 1946 and 1996.

Stage Two

In the second stage, I refined the data set to exclude advisory, quasi-official, multilateral, and educational/research agencies and support offices common to all cabinet departments. Many U.S. government agencies are advisory boards, commissions, or committees. If an agency's sole function was advisory, it was excluded from the analysis. Most advisory bodies are listed in a separate section in the *USGM* called "Boards, Commissions, and Committees." The *USGM* also includes a section for multilateral agencies, or agencies comprising representatives from both the United States and another country, such as the Asian Development Bank and the Micronesian Claims Commission. The data set excludes all multilateral agencies. The data set also excludes quasi-official government agencies (e.g., the Smithsonian Institution, the United States Institute of Peace), educational institutions (e.g., the Air Force Academy, the United States Military Academy), and research facilities (e.g., the Jet Propulsion Laboratory, the National Institute of Mental Health). Finally, I removed offices that exist in every cabinet department, such as the Office of the Inspector General or the Office of Small and Disadvantaged Business Utilization.

Stage Three

In the third stage I updated the data set for 1997 using the 1998–99 *USGM*. I then proceeded to verify and supplement the information obtained from the *USGM*. Wherever possible, I verified information in the *USGM* by examining primary sources. All pieces of legislation, executive orders, and reorganization plans are easily obtainable, and all information on agencies created by these means were double-checked for accuracy.

Reporting of internal departmental orders is haphazard. In most cases, information on agencies created by departmental orders comes from the *USGM* volume closest to their creation. There were numerous records for which the data were incomplete or missing in the *USGM*, however. For example, the Office of Marine Affairs in the Department of Interior was created on April 30, 1970, but was terminated on December 4, 1970, and was never included in the *USGM* as a regular entry. Rather, it is mentioned only in the appendix that lists agencies that have been terminated. I researched each missing case thoroughly. If these data were not available, I performed a comprehensive search of books, government documents, and law reviews for information on the missing agency. If these sources did not provide the information, I searched both the *Federal Register* (1946–97) and the *Code of Federal Regulations* (1949–97). Finally, I called and corresponded with the agencies that are still in existence or their successors for the remaining cases.

Through the process of verification and supplementing, I eliminated a number of agencies from the data set. In many cases, the missing information for an agency was its creation date. Subsequent investigation revealed that an agency was created prior to 1946. In other cases, subsequent investigation revealed that two agencies were the same organizational unit but the agency had simply been renamed. Finally, further investigation sometimes revealed that an agency was of the class (advisory bodies, institutes, etc.) removed from the data set in stage two of the data collection. The complete data set includes 438 cases. Twenty-one cases remain for which there is incomplete information. There are no cases for which no information exists. In most cases there are only a few variables with missing values. In some cases, such as the Model Cities Administration or the Office of International Finance, the only missing information is the date of the agency's termination. There remain a handful of cases for which no creation date is available. All cases with at least one missing value are listed below.

Office of International Finance—Treasury (1947)
Office of the U.S. Commissioner General Brussels Universal and
   International Exhibition (1958)
Economics and Statistics Administration—Commerce (1961)
Model Cities Administration—HUD (1966)
Alaska Power Administration (1967)
Economic Management Support Center—Agriculture (1974)
Air Force Management Engineering Agency (1975)
Air Force Medical Service Center (1985)
Air Force Manpower and Personnel Center (1985)
Wireless Telecommunications Bureau—FCC (1994)
Administration on Developmental Disabilities—HHS (?)
Administration on Native Americans—HHS (?)
Federal Telecommunications Service—GSA (?)
National Environmental Satellite, Data, and Information Service (?)
Office of Comprehensive Employment Development Programs—
   Labor (?)
Office of Grants and Program Systems—Agriculture (?)
Office of Oceanic and Atmospheric Research—NOAA (?)
Office of Space Access and Technology—NASA (?)
Office of Space Communications—NASA (?)
Office of Space Station—NASA (?)
Office of Space System Development—NASA (?)

Variables—Origination Data

1. Origin—Political actors create agencies in four different ways: by legislation, by executive order, by reorganization plan, or by departmental order. The origin variable lists the statute or executive decree that created the agency. When Congress delegates new authority, it either delegates that authority to an existing executive branch actor such as the president or a department secretary or creates a new organizational unit to implement the new mandate. Department secretaries frequently create new organizational units in response to newly delegated authority. An agency was coded as legislatively created only if the statute *requires* the creation of a new organizational unit. In a few cases Congress delegated *authority* to create a new bureau or office but did not require it. These agencies are not coded as legislatively created.

2. Origin Indicators (0,1)—The data set includes four indicator variables for the source of agency origin—one each for legislation, executive order, reorganization plan, and secretarial order. The dummy variables are mutually exclusive.

3. Date—Agencies are coded according to the year they were created. They are also coded according to their start date and their termination date. The start date for a legislatively created agency is the date the legislation is enacted. The start date for agencies created by executive order is the date the executive order is issued. Agencies created by reorganization plan have a start date equal to the date the reorganization plan becomes law. The start date for agencies created by departmental order is the date the new agency is announced. The termination dates for agencies is the date listed in appendix C of the *United States Government Manual* with the important exception that agencies whose names simply are changed are not considered terminated. Agencies that had not been terminated as of December 31, 1997, have a termination date of December 31, 1997.

Variables—Insulation Data

1. Commission Structure (0,1)—This indicator variable is coded with a 1 if an agency is headed by a board or a commission and 0 otherwise.

2. Number—This variable is a count of the number of agency administrators. Agencies without a board or commission structure are coded with a 1. All other agencies are coded according to the number of commissioners or board members.

3. Independent (0,1)—This variable is an indicator variable taking the

value of 1 if a new agency is created outside of existing bureaucratic structures. It is coded with a 0 otherwise. So the Environmental Protection Agency, which was created as an independent agency, is coded with a 1, whereas the Bureau of Alcohol, Tobacco, and Firearms, located in the Department of Treasury, is coded with a 0.

4. Term (0,1)—Agencies whose administrators serve for fixed terms are coded with a 1, and all other agencies are coded with a 0.

5. Term Length—All agencies without fixed terms are coded with a 0, and all other agencies are coded according to the length of the term.

6. Limitations on Appointment Powers (0,1)—This indicator variable is coded with a 1 if there are any explicit limitations on the type of persons that can be appointed to lead the new agency. These limitations range from the specification of past experience to limitations on the party affiliation of appointees. Any agency whose administrator(s) are appointed by any official other than the president or his subordinates is also coded with a 1.

7. Party Balancing (0,1)—This dummy variable is coded with a 1 if presidents must take party affiliation into account when making appointments to an agency. All other agencies are coded with a 0. This variable is a refinement of the limitations on appointment powers variable.

8. Location 1 (1–5)—This ordinal variable categorizes agencies according to their proximity to the president. Agencies in the Executive Office of the President (EOP) are coded with a 1. Agencies located in the cabinet are coded with a 2. Independent agencies and their component administrations, bureaus, and offices are coded with a 3. Agencies that are independent commissions or part of independent commissions are coded with a 4. Government corporations or agencies located in the legislative or judicial branch are coded with a 5.

9. Location 2 (1–5)—This variable is identical to Location 1 except that only independent commissions with a judicial or regulatory function are coded with a 4. All other independent commissions are coded with a 3.

10. Location 3 (1–5)—This variable is also identical to Location 1 except that category 4 is limited to independent regulatory commissions.

Variables—Agency Characteristics

1. Line in the Budget (0,1)—This indicator variable is coded with a 1 if the agency has an entry in the index of the *Budget of the United States Government, 1946–1999.* This determination was made by looking at the budget for the fiscal years two to three years after the creation of the agency. The budget

for 1999 was compiled in early 1998, so it is the first full budget for agencies created in 1997.

2. Budget—This is the size of an agency's budget. All agencies without a line in the budget are coded with a 0. All other agencies are coded with the size of their earliest available budget. For most agencies, the figure included is budget authority. For those agencies that have significant unexpended revenues or that generate their own revenue, such as government corporations, the figure included is the agency's total obligations.

3. GDP Deflator—This measure from the 1999 Budget of the United States Government provides a means of adjusting budget figures for inflation.

4. 1992 Budget—This measure is the size of an agency's budget adjusted to 1992 dollars.

5. Corporation (0,1)—This indicator variable is coded with a 1 if the agency is a government corporation.

6. Judicial (0,1)—This indicator variable is coded with a 1 if the agency performs an adjudicative function as one of its primary functions. The Employees Compensation Appeals Board, the Philippine War Damage Commission, and the Federal Mine Safety and Health Review Commission are examples of agencies that have an adjudicative function.

7. Trend—This term is coded with a 1 for agencies created in 1946, a 2 for agencies created in 1947, and so on.

8. Foreign Affairs (0,1)—All agencies were also coded according to their primary function or mission. There are four categories: foreign affairs, social, monetary, and general. The categories are mutually exclusive. All agencies dealing with defense, foreign affairs, and international development are coded with a 1. All other agencies are coded with a 0.

9. Social Policy (0,1)—All agencies dealing primarily with civil rights, education, benefits, health, housing, crime, aging policy, and arts are coded with a 1. All other agencies are coded with a 0.

10. Monetary (0,1)—All agencies dealing primarily with commerce, monetary policy, budgeting, banking, tax, and treasury issues are coded with a 1. All other agencies are coded with a 0.

11. General (0,1)—All agencies that were not coded with a 1 for the foreign affairs, social policy, or monetary dummy variables are coded with a 1. All other agencies are coded with a 0.

12. Foreign Affairs 2 (0,1)—This indicator variable is coded with a 1 if the agency deals primarily with foreign affairs or defense according to the coding scheme codified in the Budget Enforcement Act of 1990. All other agencies are coded with a 0.

Political Variables—Congress

1. Divided Government (0,1)—This indicator variable is coded with a 1 if different parties control the presidency and the House of Representatives or the Senate when an agency is created. All other agencies are coded with a 0.[2]

2. Size of House Majority—This is the size of the House majority as a percentage of the total chamber size when the agency was created. Its minimum is fifty and its maximum is sixty-eight.

3. Size of Senate Majority—This is the size of the Senate majority as a percentage of the total chamber size when the agency was created.

4. Length—This variable is a count of the number of elections that have passed since the majority in power last did not have a majority in both chambers of Congress.

5. Anticipation—This variable is the number of seats the majority party will retain in the House after the next election. So, for example, agencies created in 1993 or 1994 are coded with 204, since the Democratic majority in Congress lost control of the House and Senate in the 1994 midterm elections. Agencies created in 1995 or 1996 are coded with 227, since the Republican majority held this number of seats after the 1996 election.

6. Seat Trend—This variable indicates the number of seats gained or lost in the House of Representatives by the majority in the last election.

Political Variables—President

1. Approval Rating[3]—Since 1938 the Gallup Opinion Poll has asked some variant of the question "Do you approve or disapprove of the way President _____ is handling his job as president?" Each agency is coded with the percentage approving of presidential performance according to the Gallup poll taken closest to the date that an agency was created.

2. President Indicators (0,1)—These dummy variables are coded with a 1 if the agency was created during the administration of the listed president. They are coded with a 0 otherwise. There are ten dummies, and they are mutually exclusive.

3. Vetoes—This is a count of the number of regular and pocket vetoes issued in the year that an agency was created.

Miscellaneous

1. Emmerich (0,1)—This indicator variable is coded with a 1 if Emmerich 1971 lists the agency as created after 1946.

2. Whitnah (0,1)—This indicator variable is coded with a 1 if Whitnah (1983) lists the agency as created after 1946.

LIMITATIONS OF THE DATA SET

If this sample differs from a simple random sample of administrative agencies, any statistical modeling can produce biased estimates. There are three main ways that this sample could differ from a simple random sample. First, the cases with missing data are all agencies created by department secretaries or agency administrators. These agencies frequently are smaller, and the organization orders that created them are often unavailable. As a consequence, the sample of agencies included in statistical modeling will be truncated and will disproportionately include agencies created by legislation, executive orders, and reorganization plans. However, there is no evidence to suggest that the data with missing values are systematically different from other smaller agencies created by departmental orders that have no missing values. There are a large number of smaller agencies created by departmental order with no missing values, and these are probably sufficient to produce reliable and unbiased estimates.

Possibly more troubling, however, is that the sample of agencies is truncated, including only those agencies created after 1946. This can create biased estimates if the sample selected differs from other random samples of agencies selected over time. The sample of agencies created after 1946 may differ from other samples because a larger percentage of agencies are created by executive action. However, the raw number of legislatively created agencies in the sample is large enough and heterogeneous enough to provide reliable estimates, and models can include controls for the source of agency origin. As a consequence there is no reason to believe that this post-1946 sample should provide biased estimates.

Finally, it is possible that the *USGM* reports a nonrandom sample of administrative agencies. However, the *USGM* presents what most scholars would consider a comprehensive list of administrative agencies. It is possible to criticize the sample in the *USGM* because it does not mention smaller offices and programs. Sample selection of this type limits the applicability of the findings to the population of agencies important enough to be included in the *USGM*.

Appendix B

Administrative Agency Insulation
Data Set Event File

The administrative agency insulation data set has also been formatted to analyze the durability of administrative agencies with event history analysis (Tuma and Hannan 1984). Event history analysis is most easily performed if the data described in Appendix A are expanded into what is called an event file. Consider the sample from the event file shown in Table B.1.

The first column includes an agency ID. As is clear, agencies 102 and 103 have multiple records. In the complete data set each agency has one record for each year of its existence, so agencies can have as many as fifty-two records. The second column indicates the year. Agency 101 was created and terminated in 1946, so it has only one record. Since Agency 102 was created in 1946 and terminated in 1947, it has two records. Agency 103 was created in 1947 and was not terminated. The third column indicates the date that each observation begins. Each observation begins on the 1st of the year unless the agency was created during the year. If the agency was created during the year, the date listed is the agency's start date. The fourth column, end date, is the date the observation ends. Each observation ends on the last day of the year unless the agency was terminated during the year. If the agency was terminated during the year, the date listed for end date is the date the agency was terminated. The fifth and sixth columns contain data on the state of an agency. Both variables are indicator variables where 1 indicates that an agency is terminated and 0 indicates that an agency is active. In this data set all agencies begin each observation in the active state (o). They also end the observation in the active state (o) unless the agency was terminated during the year. In Table B.1, Agency 101 began the observation in an active state but ended the observation in a terminated state. Agency 102 began both observations in an active state. It ended the first observation in an active state but ended the second observation in a terminated state since it was disbanded during the year.

Agencies are also coded with time-invariant covariates and time-varying covariates. These variables provide a means of testing the impact of agency characteristics and changing political context on the durability of administrative agencies. Commission structure is an example of a time-invariant covariate. Agency 103, which is a commission, will have a value of 1 for the commission variable in each observation. Yearly average unemployment is an example of a time-varying covariate. As is clear from the last column of Table B.1, yearly average unemployment does vary over time. It changed from 3.9 to 3.8 to 5.9 between 1947 and 1949.

The event file contains all of the variables included in the flat file and a few additional variables accounting for changing political context. They are listed below.

A. Second Term (0,1)—This indicator variable is coded with a 1 if the year listed is in the second term of a president.

B. Year of Term (1–4)—This ordinal variable indicates the year of the presidential term. A president's first year is coded with a 1, his second year a 2, and so forth. Succession presidents such as Johnson and Ford are assumed to be carrying out the term of the previous president. So, for example, 1963 is coded with a 3 and 1964 is coded with a 4, even though they represent Johnson's first and second years as president.

C. War (0,1)—This is an indicator variable coded with a 1 if the United States is involved in a significant military conflict during the year. The following years are coded with a 1: 1950–53; 1965–75; 1990–91.

D. Congress—This variable indicates the Congress presiding during the year. In 1946 it was the 79th Congress, and in 1997 it was the 105th Congress.

E. Democratic House (0,1)—This indicator variable is coded with a 1 if the Democratic Party held a majority in the House of Representatives. All other years are coded with a 0.

F. Democratic Senate (0,1)—This indicator variable is coded with a 1 if the Democratic Party held a majority in the Senate. All other years are coded with a 0.

TABLE B.1

Sample of Agency Duration Spell Data

Agency ID	Year	Start Date	End Date	Starting State	Ending State	Duration (days)	Commission	Yearly Average Unemployment
101	1946	1/4/46	6/27/46	0	1	174	0	3.9
102	1946	1/22/46	12/31/46	0	0	343	0	3.9
102	1947	1/1/47	7/26/47	0	1	549	0	3.9
103	1947	7/25/47	12/31/47	0	0	159	1	3.9
103	1948	1/1/48	12/31/48	0	0	524	1	3.8
103	1949	1/1/49	12/31/49	0	0	888	1	5.9

G. Democratic President (0,1)—This indicator variable is coded with a 1 if the president is a Democrat and 0 otherwise.

H. House Majority—This variable indicates the number of seats held in the House of Representatives by the majority party.

I. Senate Majority—This variable indicates the number of seats held in the Senate by the majority party.

J. Approval Rating[1]—Since 1938 the Gallup Opinion Poll has asked some variant of the question "Do you approve or disapprove of the way President _____ is handling his job as president?" Each observation is coded with the yearly average percentage approving of presidential performance according to the Gallup poll.

K. Yearly Average Civilian Unemployment[2]—This variable indicates the yearly average civilian unemployment given by the Bureau of Labor Statistics.

L. Vetoes—This is a count of the number of public bills vetoed by the president during the year.

M. Divided Government (0,1)—This indicator variable is coded with a 1 if different parties control the presidency and the House of Representatives or the Senate during the year. All other years are coded with a 0.

N. Public Laws—This is a count of the number of laws enacted during the year.

O. House Democrats—This variable is a count of the number of Democrats in the House of Representatives.

P. House Republicans—This variable is a count of the number of Republicans in the House of Representatives.

Appendix C

Agency Data and the Possibility of Sample Selection Bias in Model Estimates

Since the data set includes only agencies *created*, the sample may differ significantly from the population of agencies *proposed*. For example, President Clinton's ill-fated health care plan would have created a new administrative agency to run the program. The plan failed, however, and the agency was never created. If we are interested in assessing the influence of presidents in the design of administrative agencies, we may be more interested in the population of proposals than the population of agencies created. The sample of administrative agencies is a subset of the population of proposals, and the subset may differ in important ways from the population of proposals. This can be a significant problem in quantitative analysis because the differences between the sample and the population can lead to bias in the estimates (see, e.g., Berk 1983). This means that we could incorrectly overestimate or underestimate the impact of certain independent variables such as presidential strength on the insulation of new administrative agencies.

In this case, however, the differences between the sample and the population of agency proposals, if it exists, is likely to lead to *underestimating* the influence of presidents. The sample likely underrepresents the number of insulated agencies proposed that are never enacted. The norm in agency design, and what predominated up until the creation of the Interstate Commerce Commission, was the creation of administrative agencies hierarchically structured under cabinet secretaries. Indeed, if no agency design is specified, an uninsulated agency is the

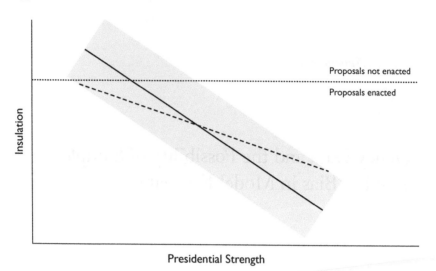

Proposals not enacted

Proposals enacted

Insulation

Presidential Strength

——— Regression line estimated from a simple random sample drawn from the population of proposals

– – – Regression line estimated from a sample of agencies actually created

FIGURE C.1   Hypothesized Effect of Sample Selection in Agency Data

default. As such, insulated agencies are a deviation from the norm that usually must be legislatively enacted. They are likely underrepresented in the sample of agencies that are actually created. Figure C.1 is a pictorial illustration of how the sample selection problem, if it exists, likely underestimates presidential influence. For the purposes of argument, assume that all proposals that fail were proposals for insulated agencies.[1] On the y axis is a hypothetical variable measuring the degree of agency insulation. On the x axis is a hypothetical variable measuring the strength of the president. The solid line represents a normal regression line estimating the relationship between presidential strength and the likelihood that a new agency will be insulated. It is estimated using a simple random sample from the population of all proposals for a new agency. The dashed line represents a different regression line estimated from the sample of agencies actually created. The sample of agencies created is quite different from the sample of the population of all proposals. It does not include all of the proposals for insulated agencies, since they are much harder to create. As a consequence, the regression line is flatter, attenuating the impact of presidential strength. The estimates from the quantitative analysis therefore could actually underestimate the impact of presidential strength.

REFERENCE MATTER

Notes

INTRODUCTION

1. For a full discussion, see Arnold 1998.
2. See Landau 1969 and Montinola n.d.
3. For a good discussion of organization problems in the executive branch and a fuller explication of what I say here, see Fesler and Kettl 1991.
4. For the Ribicoff account, see Arnold 1998. For food safety, see Freedman 1998a, 1998b. For banking regulation, see Khademian 1996.
5. For a discussion of the benefits of duplication and redundancy, see Landau 1969.
6. Of course, different structural characteristics do not affect all political actors equally. Although governance by commission dilutes political accountability for both the president and Congress, fixed terms for political appointees insulate them more from the president than from Congress. The forms of insulation I study here are primarily designed to insulate a new agency from presidential control. These forms are the most common and are the source of a large percentage of the administrative diversity in the U.S. bureaucracy.
7. See Arnold 1998.
8. See Moe 1984 for an overview.
9. See also Moe 1990a and 1990b, Moe and Caldwell 1994, and Moe and Wilson 1994.
10. Among the transaction costs the coalition tries to reduce are the costs of coming to agreement. However, no explicit mention is made of the difficulty of constructing a coalition and overcoming the many veto points in the legislative process.
11. The two literatures dealing with agency design, that focusing on delegation and that focusing on insulation, use different language when describing the process, and this can lead to confusion. The first seeks to explain how Congress can delegate authority to an administrative agency and ensure that the agency produces the types of public policy outputs the congressional majority prefers both today and in the future. When members of Congress worry about the divergent preferences of the administrative actor, they reduce the amount

of *discretion* this actor will have. They write very specific statutes, implement budgetary devices like automatic cost-of-living increases, or design administrative procedures that ensure the participation of the relevant interests in agency decision making (Epstein and O'Halloran 1999; Horn 1995; McCubbins, Noll, and Weingast 1987, 1989).

The second literature is less concerned about the congressional delegation decision. Instead, it is concerned with control and the impediments to political control (Moe 1985). It explains when political actors will *insulate* administrative agencies from political control (Moe 1989, 1990b; Moe and Wilson 1994). Both literatures are examining the same political process, one talking about discretion and the other about insulation. Discretion and insulation are related concepts. When Congress decreases the discretion of administrative agencies, it is insulating the agency from political influence. Future political actors cannot change the direction of the agency because the agency's actions are carefully circumscribed.

Part of the confusion between the two literatures is due to different levels of analyses. Take, for example, the Federal Reserve. Most scholars argue that Congress has delegated to the Board of Governors of the Federal Reserve a large amount of authority with very few constraints. In short, the board has a lot of discretion. At the same time, those scholars studying insulation argue that the Federal Reserve was designed to be insulated from political control. Can the Federal Reserve have lots of discretion and be insulated? The answer depends upon the level of analysis. If, on the one hand, scholars are analyzing administrative agencies, the Federal Reserve has a tremendous amount of discretion. If, on the other hand, scholars are analyzing the executive branch, the president has much less discretion, because the Federal Reserve is insulated from his control. Congress could decrease the discretion of both the administrative agency and the president by writing more specific statutes or restrictive administrative procedures.

12. Moe and William G. Howell do an excellent job explaining presidential advantages arising from the president's ability to act as a unitary actor and take advantage of Congress's inability to come to agreement (Howell 2000; Howell and Lewis 2002; Moe and Howell 1998; Moe and Wilson 1994).

13. Indeed, no research to date has analyzed the creation of administrative agencies with quantitative data. Moe (1989) and Moe and Wilson (1994) present a series of case studies intended to illustrate the political nature of agency design and the presidential advantages in agency design, respectively. Murray Horn (1995) and Amy Beth Zegart (1999) also test their theories of agency design with a series of case studies. Only David Epstein and Sharyn O'Halloran (1996, 1999)

attempt to validate the derivations of their models with quantitative data. Consistent with their focus on congressional delegation, however, their analysis neither examines agency design nor includes any measures of presidential influence.

14. See Moe 1989 and Zegart 1999, who focus more on actors I omit.

CHAPTER 1

1. Another way of discussing Congress's capacity to come to agreement is to examine the divergence of member preferences within and between chambers. If there is broad disagreement among members, it is less likely that a proposed bill will pass both chambers, survive a filibuster, and escape a veto. As such, we could measure Congress's raw ability to coalesce by examining the divergence of preferences within and across chambers.

2. If this majority is about to lose power, this also may factor in to the desire to insulate.

CHAPTER 2

1. That is, those agencies created by legislation and listed in the *United States Government Manual* during this period.

2. Most of the empirical work on political insulation has been limited to case studies (see, e.g., Horn 1995; McCubbins, Noll, and Weingast 1989; Moe 1989). The only quantitative work in this area is by David Epstein and Sharyn O'Halloran (1999). The focus of their analysis, like that of most of the literature in this area, is the congressional delegation decision rather than the design of administrative agencies. The part of the analysis that comes closest to the question here is the attempt to determine where Congress will delegate new authority. Will it be delegated to relatively uninsulated agencies such as those in the Executive Office of the President (EOP) or cabinet, or to more insulated agencies such as independent commissions or government corporations? Their analysis suggests that Congress is more likely to delegate to insulated administrative agencies during divided government.

3. A full description of the construction of the data set and coding decisions is included in Appendix A.

4. See Davidson and Oleszek 1994.

5. Just this issue was contested in *Mistretta v. United States*, 488 U.S. 361 (1989). The court ruled that the location of this body in the judicial branch did not violate the separation of powers provided in the Constitution.

6. I borrow this idea from Epstein and O'Halloran 1999.

7. The bill also made the director of the Park Service subject to Senate confirmation, required professional experience for all appointees, created a three-

member National Park System review board to review existing and proposed parks, and provided that the director provide information directly to Congress without review by the secretary of interior. Although the bill passed the House of Representatives in both 1988 and 1989, the Senate never acted on the bill (*Congressional Quarterly Almanac* 1988, 148–49; *Congressional Quarterly Almanac* 1989, 693–94).

8. Among the different types of nonstatutory controls are committee reports, floor arguments, informal agreements, oversight, and hearings. These usually carry with them an informal threat of congressional action should the agency refuse to comply. Still, they do not carry the weight of law and are frequently disobeyed (Kirst 1969).

9. Source: Nelson 1996. Updated from Gallup Web site (http://www.gallup.com).

10. Perhaps a more obvious measure of congressional durability would be whether the president is in his first or second term. The difficulty with employing this measure, however, is that there were no second-term presidents in unified government during this period, making it difficult to disentangle the effects of divided government from presidential durability. Those models estimated only during divided government with an indicator for second term confirm what is reported here. I have also estimated models using year of the term to measure presidential durability, and they generally confirm what is reported here.

11. Specifically I used an agency's budget at the time it was created (adjusted for inflation) if it had a line in the budget. This specification has the advantage of more accurately measuring agency size, but the disadvantage of including fewer cases. Since not all agencies have a line in the budget, budget data for these observations are missing.

12. I have also estimated models using different variations of the agency location measure. I estimated models including indicator variables for location outside the cabinet (0,1) and location in an independent commission (0,1). These models confirm what is reported in the text. I also estimated a multinomial logit model, which assumes no ordering among the five categories, of the agency location measure. The results of this model confirm what is reported in the text with the exception that presidential durability has no impact on the relative probability a new agency is placed in the cabinet or some other location in the bureaucracy.

13. I use the robust estimator of variance proposed by P. J. Huber (1967) and H. White (1980, 1982), adjusted for clustering on years (see Rogers 1993), to calculate standard errors. I have also estimated models without the robust estimator of variance, with the robust estimator of variance but no adjustment for clus-

tering, and random effects probit models. The results confirm what is reported in the main text. The results are robust to the type of model and means of estimating the standard errors. The formula for the robust estimator of variance is

$$\hat{v} = \hat{v}(\sum_{j=1}^{N} u_j' u_j)\hat{v}$$

where $\hat{v} = (-\partial^2 \ln L / \partial \beta^2)^{-1}$ and u_j is the contribution from the jth observation to the scores $\partial \ln L / \partial \beta$. If the observations are not independent, however, we can assume that the j observations can be divided into M groups $G_1, G_2, \ldots$ G_M that are independent. The estimator of variance becomes

$$\hat{v} = \hat{V} (\sum_{j=1}^{N} u_j^{(G)'} u_j^{(G)})\hat{V}$$

where $u_k^{(G)}$ is the contribution of the kth group, (k=1, . . . ,M), to the scores $\partial \ln L / \partial \beta$. If the log likelihood adds the j observations,

$$\ln L = \sum_{j=1}^{N} \ln L_j$$

then $u_j = \partial \ln L_j / \partial \beta$ and this implies that

$$u_k^{(G)} = \sum_{j \in G_k}^{N} u_j$$

So the group scores are simply sums of the individual scores within each group. In this context the groups are years. This is taken directly from Stata Statistical Software (StataCorp 1997, 239).

14. All models were estimated in Stata 6.0 for PC. All simulations were calculated in Microsoft Excel 2000.

Since the data set includes only agencies created, the sample may differ significantly from the population of agencies proposed. For a full discussion of the possibility of sample selection bias, see Appendix C.

15. All simulations are run assuming that an agency has a line in the budget and the trend term is set at its mean value, twenty-three years.

16. An additional difficulty is that the measures of majority strength are really imperfect measures of Congress's ability to come to agreement. I have tried to use other measures of congressional capacity, such as major pieces of legislation enacted by each Congress, size of Senate majority, and preference divergence within and between chambers, and the results generally confirm the findings here. When Congress wants to constrain the president, its strength, ability to come to agreement, or capacity really matters.

Notes

CHAPTER 3

1. For a good overview of presidential attitudes toward reorganization, see Arnold 1998.

2. See Clinton et al. 1999 and McCarty 1999.

3. The president has the added advantage in foreign policy of additional formal powers. The Constitution empowers the president as commander in chief and gives the office the power to receive ambassadors and negotiate treaties. In modern times, these powers have evolved to mean the power to commit troops, the power to recognize foreign governments, and the power to issue executive agreements and unilaterally terminate treaty arrangements.

4. Indeed, with regard to the power to commit troops, Alexander Hamilton, John Jay, and James Madison lauded the new Constitution for its *constraints* on the ability of the executive to make war. In *Federalist 69* Hamilton notes that although kings have the power to declare war and raise and regulate navies and armies, these powers have purposefully been given to Congress by the Constitution. Jay notes in *Federalist 4* that kings make war for personal reasons, such as thirst for military glory, revenge, or personal affront. He contrasts this, however, with the Constitution, which proscribes the ability of the executive to make wars apart from popular support. Madison, in his writings, says, "Those who are to conduct a war cannot in the nature of things, be proper or safe judges, whether a war ought to be commenced, continued or concluded."

5. For full discussion of presidential unilateral action, see Howell 2003, Howell and Lewis 2002, Mayer 2001, Moe and Howell 1999, and Moe and Wilson 1994.

6. For excellent discussions of presidents and civil rights, see Graham 1992, Howell 2003, Mayer 2001, and Morgan 1970.

7. More recently, President Clinton used the 1906 Antiquities Act in 1996 to create a national monument out of the 1.7 million–acre Grand Staircase property in southern Utah. The Republican majority in Congress has responded by attempting to pass legislation to subject presidential decisions under the act to more public scrutiny and comment.

8. The comptroller general testified in 1970 that "as a practical matter, if the expenses of the groups are justified in the budget presentations, this is regarded as being adequate for this purpose. When they say specific authorization by Congress, authorization is usually meant to be approved through the appropriation process if not through the regular legislative authorization process. In other words, it does not have to be specifically authorized by separate statute" (U.S. House 1970, 39).

9. Continued misuse of these discretionary funds, however, has led to more restrictions and reductions over time. As Representative John Rhodes (R-Ariz.) said, "Unfortunately, I think it is a matter of public knowledge that in many instances this contingency fund has been used for one contingency only and that contingency is that the House and Senate did not appropriate as much money for this program as the people downtown would like to have appropriated" (*Cong. Rec.* 1961, 107, pt. 10:21477).

CHAPTER 4

1. That is, agencies large enough to be included in the *United States Government Manual* and excluding advisory agencies, multilateral agencies, and educational and research institutions.

2. This may reflect some source bias since *Congress and the Nation* is an almanac focusing on legislative affairs.

3. The National Biological Service was originally called the National Biological Survey. The secretary changed its name by Department Order 3185, issued January 5, 1995. The secretary subsequently changed the name one more time to the Life Sciences Research Bureau. Both name changes were made in an attempt to deflect attention from the service's role in carrying out the Endangered Species Act and to highlight its role as the basic science bureau of the Department of Interior (NBS 1995; Kenworthy 1995).

4. U.S. House 1993a, 30; see also Pulliam 1995.

5. U.S. Department of Interior 1993. Reorganization Plan 3 of 1950 had transferred to the secretary almost all authority previously delegated to subordinate officials in the Interior Department. It also granted the secretary substantial discretion in shaping the administrative organization of the department. The relevant sections of the reorganization plan, sections 2 and 5, read as follows:

Sec. 2. The Secretary of the Interior may from time to time make such provisions as he shall deem appropriate authorizing the performance by any other officer, or by any agency or employee, of the Department of the Interior of any function of the Secretary, including any function transferred to the Secretary by the provisions of this reorganization plan. . . .

Sec. 5. The Secretary of the Interior may from time to time effect such transfers within the Department of the Interior of any of the records, property, personnel, and unexpended balances (available or to be made available) of appropriations, allocations, and other funds of such Department as he may deem necessary in order to carry out the provisions of this reorganization plan.

As such, there was general agreement that the secretary had the authority to create the NBS and reshuffle existing departmental administrative arrangements.

6. Order 3173 stipulated that the order creating the NBS would not become effective until the establishment of budget authority for the NBS. Since 1946 all new agencies have had to obtain authorization from Congress within two years of their creation to spend appropriated funds. In 1946, in response to President Roosevelt's unilateral creation of the Fair Employment Practices Commission, Congress passed the Russell Amendment, requiring that all agencies created by executive order obtain formal authorization within two years of their creation. The statute on its face appears to require new agencies to receive either a statutory authorization or a specific appropriation by Congress. The amendment, however, has been interpreted in practice to only require that a new agency's existence be justified in larger budget presentations. The comptroller general testified in 1970 that "as a practical matter, if the expenses of the groups are justified in the budget presentations, this is regarded as being adequate for this purpose. When they say specific authorization by Congress, authorization is usually meant to be approved through the appropriation process if not through the regular legislative authorization process. In other words, it does not have to be specifically authorized by separate statute" (U.S. House 1970, 39).

7. The issue of formal authorization was specifically mentioned in a number of congressional hearings. The NBS's opponents acknowledged that, while they opposed the creation of an agency with no explicit authorization, the administration had the legal right to do so (U.S. House 1993a, 30, 41–42).

8. See U.S. House 1993a, 41; *Congressional Quarterly Almanac* 1993, 269–70; Corn 1995.

9. For both quotations, see Pulliam 1998a, 1998b.

10. Kenworthy 1995; see also U.S. House 1995, 3.

11. 110 *STAT* 1321-165-6; U.S. Department of Interior 1996.

12. Personal communication with H. Ron Pulliam, director of the NBS, May 10, 2000.

13. Variables that count the number of times something has happened are frequently modeled with Poisson regression. Poisson regression models assume that the conditional variance is equal to the conditional mean. This is rarely true in practice. In negative binomial regression models, an additional parameter is added that allows the conditional variance to exceed the conditional mean. Poisson models are a special case of negative binomial models where the ancillary parameter (or dispersion parameter), α, equals zero. A likelihood ra-

tio test of nested models can determine whether the inclusion of the ancillary parameter significantly improves the model. See Long 1997.

14. The Central Security Service, for example, was created in December 1971 and did not appear in the *United States Government Manual* until 1974. I also estimated models for the complete 1946–97 period with the knowledge that the 1996–97 data might be incomplete. The results were significantly weaker. Although the signs remained in the expected direction, several coefficients lost significance.

15. The Korean War (1950–53), the Vietnam War (1965–75), and the Persian Gulf War (1990–91) years are coded 1 and all other years are coded 0. Average yearly unemployment is 5.67 percent, with a low of 2.9 (1953) and a high of 9.7 (1982); the standard deviation is 1.58. All years in which a Democrat served in the White House are coded 1, and all other years are coded with a 0. I have also estimated models with Poole (1998) common space scores for presidents. Since the Poole scores only go back to Eisenhower, I use Truman's common space score as a senator. The results from the models are the same. All years in which the same party did not control both chambers of Congress and the White House are coded 1, and all other years 0.

16. This is true unless, for some reason, small majorities always prefer more uninsulated agencies. There is no theoretical reason why this should be true. If, on the other hand, large majorities always prefer an uninsulated agency, which seems more reasonable, then the coefficient on majority size should be positive and significant.

CHAPTER 5

1. For a summary of the classified and unclassified reports, see President's Foreign Intelligence Advisory Board 1999. My discussion on the history of security lapses at the DOE and early administration responses to these revelations relies heavily on this report.

2. See Freedberg 1999, 1896, and President's Foreign Intelligence Advisory Board 1999.

3. The board was commissioned by President Clinton on March 18, 1999, to report on "the security threat at the Department of Energy's weapons labs and the adequacy of the measures that have been taken to address it" (President's Foreign Intelligence Advisory Board 1999).

4. President's Foreign Intelligence Advisory Board 1999, 39–41. See also Risen 1999.

5. Cox actually preferred an independent agency like the defunct Atomic

Notes

Energy Commission. For Cox's view, see Pincus and Loeb 1999. For Packard's view, see McCutcheon 1999d.

6. There are reports that suggest that Richardson himself persuaded Clinton to appoint him interim head of the NNSA. See, e.g., *CQ Weekly* 1999, 2866.

7. U.S. House 2000a. See also McCutcheon 2000b.

8. See U.S. House 2000b; McCutcheon 2000d.

9. I have also estimated models using a measure of seats in the Senate and a measure of seats in whichever chamber held the larger percentage of the president's party. The results corroborate what is reported here.

10. These simulations are conducted using a hypothetical domestic agency created by statute during unified government when the party size and presidential approval are at their mean unless otherwise specified.

CHAPTER 6

1. Secretary's memorandum 1010-1, October 20, 1994. As listed in the 1998–99 *United States Government Manual*, p. 767.

2. Presidents argue, of course, that removing agencies from presidential control produces other inefficiencies. Presidents lose their ability to rationalize and coordinate executive branch activities, leading to overlapping responsibilities, unclear jurisdiction, and agency coordination problems (Arnold 1998; Emmerich 1971; Lewis 2000; Moe 1989, 1990a; Moe and Wilson 1994).

3. Kaufman examines agencies in existence in 1923 and finds a termination rate for that cohort of around 15 percent. Of the 421 agencies he examines overall (in 1923 and 1973), 27 were terminated. Since the data set excludes agencies created prior to 1923 and terminated prior to 1923 and excludes agencies created after 1923 and terminated prior to 1973, however, the sample is biased toward durable agencies. Kaufman's data also include only agencies from executive departments.

4. The nonparametric maximum likelihood estimate of the survivor function suggested by Kaplan and Meier (1958) is:

$$\hat{S}(t) = \prod_{i|t_i \le t} \left(\frac{n_i - d_i}{n_i} \right)$$

where n_t is the population alive at time t and d_t is the number of failures at time t.

5. This result is confirmed by a log-rank test of the equality of the survivor functions, which allows us to reject the null hypothesis that the survivor functions are equal ($p < .00$, 4 df). A log-rank test of the equality of the survivor

functions of agencies in the cabinet and agencies in independent administrations indicates that we cannot reject the null hypothesis that the survivor functions for the two types of agencies are equal (p < .16, 1 df).

6. Log-rank tests of the equality of the survivor functions support these conclusions. We can reject the null hypothesis that agencies without the insulating characteristics have the same survivor function as agencies with the insulating characteristics (p < .00, 1 df). The only exception is for agencies with commission structures. We cannot reject the null hypothesis that the survivor function for these agencies is the same as that for agencies without commission structures (p < .81).

7. The functional form of the baseline hazard rate has been the subject of some debate in the discipline recently. Andrew Eric Newman (1991) and Daniel Carpenter (2000) argue that the baseline hazard rate is nonmonotonic. In order to verify the robustness of the results to different specifications, I have also estimated semiparametric Cox proportional hazard models and parametric models specifying log-normal or log-logistic forms for $q(t)$. Other than minor differences in the impact of the different independent variables, the results are virtually identical to those presented in Table 6.1.

8. Sources: *Information Please Almanac*, various years; *Historical Statistics of the United States* 1989; *Handbook of Labor Statistics* 1989; Bureau of Labor Statistics Web site (http://www.dol.gov).

9. All analyses were performed in Inter-cooled STATA 6.0 for PC. Since the data set has multiple observations on one subject, it is possible that the observations are not independent. As a consequence, I have also estimated the models with a robust estimator of variance to account for correlation of the errors in observations on the same agency. The results confirm what is reported in the main text.

10. In particular, the measures of independence and governance by board or commission are highly collinear with the independent administration (3) and the independent commission (4) categories of the location measure. Nonetheless, when a model was estimated with the location measure and the indicators of insulation, the results confirm what is reported here.

11. Another observationally equivalent possibility is that the shape of the hazard rate reflects a sorting process in which only weak agencies are terminated.

12. To interpret the impact of the coefficients on the hazard rate of agency mortality, we must remember that $\Theta(x) = \exp(\beta'x) = \Pi \lambda_j^{x_j}$ where $\lambda_j = \exp(\beta_j)$. A common interpretation of x_j is that if it has no impact on $h(t)$, then $\beta_j = 0$ and $\lambda_j = 1$ The percentage change in the hazard rate associated with a unit

Notes

change in x_j = 100 * $(\lambda_j - 1)$. So, for example, if β_j = 0.25, then λ_j = exp(.25) = 1.28 and a one-unit increase in x_j increases the hazard rate, $h(t)$, by 100 * (1.28 − 1) = 28 percent. This is taken directly from Tuma (n.d.).

APPENDIX A

1. The data set includes all agencies listed in the *United States Government Manual* (*USGM*) index or appendix of terminated agencies. As discussed below, the data set excludes advisory, quasi-official, multilateral, educational, and research agencies and support offices common to all cabinet departments. The data set also excludes agencies listed in the *USGM* but not mentioned in the index or appendix.

2. All political variables relating to Congress come from Ornstein, Mann, and Malbin 1998.

3. Source: Nelson 1996. *Gallup Opinion Index*, various years (Gallup Web site: http://www.gallup.com).

APPENDIX B

1. Source: Nelson 1996. *Gallup Opinion Index*, various years (Gallup Web site: http://www.gallup.com).

2. Sources: *Information Please Almanac*, various years; *Historical Statistics of the United States* 1989; Bureau of Labor Statistics Web site (http://www.dol.gov).

APPENDIX C

1. Of course, not all proposals for agencies that fail are proposals for insulated agencies. For the sample to underestimate the president's influence, however, the sample simply has to be more likely to exclude insulated agencies than noninsulated agencies.

Bibliography

Arnold, Peri E. 1998. *Making the managerial presidency: Comprehensive reorganization planning, 1905–1996.* Lawrence: University Press of Kansas.

Bawn, Kathleen. 1995. "Political control versus expertise: Congressional choices about administrative procedures." *American Political Science Review* 89:62.

———. 1997. "Choosing strategies to control the bureaucracy: Statutory constraints, oversight, and the committee system." *Journal of Law, Economics, and Organization* 13:101–26.

Becker, Elizabeth, and Elaine Sciolino. 2001. "A new federal office opens amid concerns it won't have enough power." *New York Times*, October 8, late edition, section B, p. 11.

Benze, James G., Jr. 1985. "Presidential reorganization as a tactical weapon: Putting politics back into administration." *Presidential Studies Quarterly* 15:145–57.

Berk, Richard A. 1983. "An introduction to sample selection bias in sociological data." *American Sociological Review* 48:386–98.

Bernstein, Marver H. 1977. *Regulating business by independent commission.* Westport, Conn.: Greenwood Press.

Brady, David W., and Craig Volden. 1998. *Revolving gridlock: Politics and policy from Carter to Clinton.* Boulder, Colo.: Westview Press.

Brody, Richard A. 1991. *Assessing the president: The media, elite opinion, and public support.* Stanford, Calif.: Stanford University Press.

Bruderl, Josef, Peter Preisendorfer, and Rolf Ziegler. 1992. "Survival chances of newly founded business organizations." *American Sociological Review* 57:227.

Burke, John P. 1992. *The institutional presidency.* Baltimore, Md.: Johns Hopkins University Press.

Canes-Wrone, Brandice. 1999. "Essays in executive branch policy influence." Ph.D. dissertation, Stanford University.

Canes-Wrone, Brandice, and Scott DeMarchi. 2002. "Presidential approval and legislative success." *Journal of Politics* 64:491–509.

Canes-Wrone, Brandice, William G. Howell, David E. Lewis, and Terry M. Moe. 1999. "The two presidencies in the legislative and executive arenas."

Paper presented at annual meeting of the Midwest Political Science Association, Chicago, Ill.

Carpenter, Daniel P. 2000. "Stochastic prediction and estimation of nonlinear political durations: An application to the lifetime of bureaus." In *Political complexity: Nonlinear models of politics*, edited by Diana Richards, pp. 209–38. Ann Arbor: University of Michigan Press.

Clayton, Cornell. 1992. *The politics of justice: The attorney general and the making of legal policy*. Armonk, N.Y.: M. E. Sharpe.

Clinton, Joshua D., David E. Lewis, Stephanie K. Riegg, and Barry Weingast. 1999. "Strategically speaking: The three strategies of going public." Paper presented at annual meeting of the American Political Science Association, Atlanta, Ga.

Clinton, William J. 1993. *Remarks for Earth Day*. April 21, U.S. Botanical Gardens, Washington, D.C.

———. 1999a. *Press conference by the president*. Presidential Hall, June 25.

———. 1999b. Statement on signing the National Defense Authorization Act for fiscal year 2000. *Weekly Compilation of Presidential Documents*, vol. 35, no. 40, p. 1887.

Congress and the Nation: 1945–1964. 1998. Vols. 1A and 1B. (Washington, D.C.: CQ Press).

Congress and the Nation: 1965–1968. 1969. Vol. 2. (Washington, D.C.: CQ Press).

Congress and the Nation: 1973–1976. 1977. Vol. 4. (Washington, D.C.: CQ Press).

Congress and the Nation: 1993–1996. 1998. Vol. 9. (Washington, D.C.: CQ Press).

Congressional Quarterly Almanac. 1966. (Washington, D.C.: CQ Press).

Congressional Quarterly Almanac. 1988. (Washington, D.C.: CQ Press).

Congressional Quarterly Almanac. 1989. (Washington, D.C.: CQ Press).

Congressional Quarterly Almanac. 1993. (Washington, D.C.: CQ Press).

Congressional Quarterly Almanac. 1994. (Washington, D.C.: CQ Press).

Congressional Quarterly Almanac. 1995. (Washington, D.C.: CQ Press).

Congressional Record. 1937. 75th Cong., 1st sess., vol. 81, pt. 6.

Congressional Record. 1961. 87th Cong., 1st sess., vol. 107, pt. 10.

Corn, M. Lynne. 1995. *The National Biological Service*. Congressional research service report for Congress.

CQ Weekly. 1999. "Nuclear Security." November 27, p. 2866.

Cushman, John H., Jr. 1995. "Timber! A new idea is crashing." *New York Times*, January 22, sec. 4, p. 5.

Cushman, Robert Eugene. 1972. *The independent regulatory commissions.* New York: Octagon Books.

Daniels, Mark Ross. 1997. *Terminating public programs: An American political paradox.* Armonk, N.Y.: M. E. Sharpe.

Davidson, Roger H., and Walter J. Oleszek. 1994. *Congress and Its Members.* Washington, D.C.: CQ Press.

Department of Energy. 2000a. "Energy department proceeds with implementation of National Nuclear Security Administration." *Department of Energy News Release,* January 7.

Derthick, Martha. 1990. *Agency under stress: The Social Security Administration in American government.* Washington, D.C.: Brookings Institution.

Downs, Anthony. 1967. *Inside bureaucracy.* Boston: Little Brown.

Emmerich, Herbert. 1971. *Federal organization and administrative management.* University, Ala.: University of Alabama Press.

Epstein, David, and Sharyn O'Halloran. 1994. "Administrative procedures, information, and agency discretion." *American Journal of Political Science* 38:697–722.

———. 1996. "Divided government and the design of administrative procedures: A formal model and empirical test." *Journal of Politics* 58:373.

———. 1999. *Delegating powers: A transaction cost politics approach to policy making under separate powers.* New York: Cambridge University Press.

Fesler, James W., and Donald F. Kettl. 1991. *The politics of the administrative process.* Chatham, N.J.: Chatham House.

Fiorina, Morris P. 1986. "Legislator uncertainty, legislative control, and the delegation of legislative power." *Journal of Law, Economics, and Organization* 2:33–51.

Fisher, Louis. 1975. *Presidential spending power.* Princeton, N.J.: Princeton University Press.

———. 1998. *The politics of shared power: Congress and the executive.* College Station: Texas A&M University Press.

———. 2000. "Congressional abdication on war and spending." College Station: Texas A&M University Press.

Foerstel, Karen. 1999. "House panel approves INS breakup." *CQ Weekly,* November 6, p. 2656.

Fox, William F. 1997. *Understanding administrative law.* New York: Matthew Bender.

Freedberg, Sydney J., Jr. 1999. "Energy lab debate boils over." *National Journal* 31(26): 1896–97.

Freedman, Allan. 1998a. "Battles over jurisdiction likely to block merger of agencies." *CQ Weekly*, May 30, p. 1440.

Freedman, Allan. 1998b. "Unsafe food sparks outbreaks of concern, little action." *CQ Weekly*, May 30, pp. 1436–41.

Freeman, John, Glenn R. Carroll, and Michael T. Hannan. 1983. "The liability of newness: Age dependence in organizational death rates." *American Sociological Review* 48:692–710.

Gellhorn, Walter. 1987. *Administrative law: Cases and comments*. Mineola, N.Y.: Foundation Press.

"GOP proposal for DOE shakeup runs aground on Democratic reef." 1999. Associated Press Newswires, May 28.

Graham, Hugh Davis. 1992. *Civil rights and the presidency*. New York: Oxford University Press.

Gugliotta, Guy. 1995. "On the list: Survivors and newcomers: At agencies slated for termination, officials remain hopeful but mindful of pressure." *Washington Post*, May 11, p. A6.

Handbook of Labor Statistics, 1989. 1989. Washington, D.C.: GPO.

Historical Statistics of the United States: From Colonial Times to 1970. 1989. Kraus.

Hoff, Samuel B. 1991. "Saying no: Presidential support and veto use, 1889–1988." *American Politics Quarterly* 19:310–23.

Horn, Murray J. 1995. *The political economy of public administration: Institutional choice in the public sector*. New York: Cambridge University Press.

Howell, William G. 2000. "The presidential power of unilateral action." Ph.D. dissertation, Stanford University.

———. 2003. *Power without persuasion: A theory of presidential action*. Princeton, N.J.: Princeton University Press.

Howell, William G., and David E. Lewis. 2002. "Agencies by presidential design." *Journal of Politics* 64:1095–1114.

Huber, John D., Charles R. Shipan, and Madelaine Pfahler. 2001. "Legislatures and statutory control of the bureaucracy." *American Journal of Political Science* 45:330–45.

Huber, P. J. 1967. "The behavior of maximum likelihood estimates under nonstandard conditions." Paper presented at Fifth Berkeley Symposium in Mathematical Statistics and Probability, Berkeley, Calif.

Hult, Karen M. 1987. *Agency merger and bureaucratic redesign*. Pittsburgh: University of Pittsburgh Press.

Johnson, Lyndon B. 1966. *Public papers of the presidents of the United States: Lyndon B. Johnson, 1963–1969*. 10 vols. Washington, D.C.: GPO.

Kaplan, E. L., and P. Meier. 1958. "Non-parametric estimation for incomplete observations." *Journal of the American Statistical Association* 53:457–81.

Kaufman, Herbert. 1976. *Are government organizations immortal?* Washington, D.C.: Brookings Institution.

Kenworthy, Tom. 1995. "By any name, Biological Service appears to be endangered species." *Washington Post*, June 27, A15.

Khademian, Anne M. 1996. *Checking on banks: Autonomy and accountability in three federal agencies*. Washington, D.C.: Brookings Institution Press.

King, Gary. 1993. "Methodology and the presidency." In *Researching the presidency*, edited by George C. Edwards III, John H. Kessel, and Bert A. Rockman, pp. 387–412. Pittsburgh: University of Pittsburgh Press.

Kirst, Michael W. 1969. *Government without passing laws: Congress' nonstatutory techniques for appropriations control*. Chapel Hill: University of North Carolina Press.

Koffler, Keith. 2001. "Bush makes plea to Graham on homeland security position." *Congress Daily*, October 25. (www.nationaljournal.com).

Krehbiel, Keith. 1998. *Pivotal politics: A theory of U.S. lawmaking*. Chicago: University of Chicago Press.

Kurian, George T., ed. 1998. *A Historical Guide to the U.S. Government*. New York: Oxford University Press.

Landau, Martin. 1969. "Redundancy, rationality, and the problem of duplication and overlap." *Public Administration Review* 29 (July/August): 346–58.

Lewis, David E. 2000. "Presidents and the politics of agency design: Political insulation in the United States government bureaucracy, 1946–1997." Ph.D. dissertation, Stanford University.

———. 2002. "The politics of agency termination: confronting the myth of agency immortality." *Journal of Politics* 64:89–107.

Lewis, David E., and James Michael Strine. 1996. "What time is it? The use of power in four different types of presidential time." *Journal of Politics* 58:682.

Long, J. Scott. 1997. *Regression models for categorical and limited dependent variables*. Thousand Oaks, Calif.: Sage Publications.

Lowi, Theodore J. 1979. *The end of liberalism: The second republic of the United States*. New York: Norton.

———. 1985. *The personal president: Power invested, promise unfulfilled*. Ithaca, N.Y.: Cornell University Press.

Macey, Jonathan R. 1992. "Organizational design and the political control of administrative agencies." *Journal of Law, Economics, and Organization* 8:93–110.

Mackenzie, G. Calvin. 1981. *The Politics of presidential appointments.* New York: Free Press.

Mayer, Ken. 2001. *With the stroke of a pen.* Princeton, N.J.: Princeton University Press.

Mayhew, David R. 1974. *Congress: The electoral connection.* New Haven, Conn.: Yale University Press.

McCarty, Nolan. 1999. "Bargaining over authority: The case of the appointment power." Paper presented at annual meeting of the American Political Science Association, Atlanta, Ga.

McCubbins, Mathew D. 1985. "The legislative design of regulatory structure." *American Journal of Political Science* 29:721–48.

McCubbins, Mathew D., Roger Noll, and Barry Weingast. 1987. "Administrative procedures as instruments of political control." *Journal of Law, Economics, and Organization* 3:243–77.

———. 1989. "Structure and process, politics and policy: Administrative arrangements and the political control of agencies." *Virginia Law Review* 75:431–82.

McCubbins, Mathew D., and Thomas Schwartz. 1984. "Congressional oversight overlooked: Police patrol versus fire alarm." *American Journal of Political Science* 32:165–77.

McCutcheon, Chuck. 1999a. "House takes a step to strengthen protection of defense technology." *CQ Weekly*, June 12, pp. 1392–94.

———. 1999b. "Proposal for a nuclear security agency gains momentum with lawmakers." *CQ Weekly*, June 19, pp. 1475–76.

———. 1999c. "Meetings with Berger, Richardson fail to quell senators' concerns about nuclear security leaks." *CQ Weekly*, July 3, p. 1633.

———. 1999d. "House bill would slash funds for Energy Department, give boost to water projects." *CQ Weekly*, July 17, pp. 1729–30.

———. 1999e. "Senate, White House agree on a new nuclear agency as House studies options." *CQ Weekly*, July 24, pp. 1811–12.

———. 1999f. "GOP, Richardson eyeball to eyeball over nuclear security again, with little time left for a blink." *CQ Weekly*, October 23, p. 2537.

———. 2000a. "Nuclear agency plan goes to hill." *CQ Weekly*, January 8, p. 61.

———. 2000b. "DOE's nuclear agency proposal meets criticism on the hill." *CQ Weekly*, January 15, p. 92.

———. 2000c. "Panel accuses Energy Department of trying to run nuclear agency." *CQ Weekly*, February 12, p. 329.

———. 2000d. "Security boast at energy 'nonsense.'" *CQ Weekly*, February 19, p. 372.

———. 2000e. "Members praise nominee for new weapons agency, remain critical of 'dual-hatting.'" *CQ Weekly*, March 4, p. 486.

———. 2000d. "Hill takes hands-on approach to tightening nuclear security." *CQ Weekly*, July 1, p. 1619.

———. 2001. "Defining homeland security." *CQ Weekly*, September 30, pp. 2252–54.

Moe, Terry M. 1982. "Regulatory performance and presidential administration." *American Journal of Political Science* 26:197–224.

———. 1984. "The new economics of organization." *American Political Science Review* 28:739–77.

———. 1985. "The politicized presidency." In *The New Direction in American Politics*, edited by John E. Chubb and Paul E. Peterson. Washington, D.C.: Brookings Institution Press.

———. 1989. "The politics of bureaucratic structure." In *Can the Government Govern?* edited by John E. Chubb and Paul E. Peterson. Washington, D.C.: Brookings Institution Press.

———. 1990a. "Political institutions: The neglected side of the story." *Journal of Law, Economics, and Organization* 6:213–53.

———. 1990b. "The politics of structural choice: Toward a theory of public bureaucracy." In *Organization theory: From Chester Barnard to the present and beyond*, edited by O. E. Williamson. New York: Oxford University Press.

Moe, Terry M., and Michael Caldwell. 1994. "The institutional foundations of democratic government: A comparison of presidential and parliamentary systems." *Journal of Institutional and Theoretical Economics* 150(1):171–95.

Moe, Terry M., and William G. Howell. 1998. "The presidential power of unilateral action." Paper presented at *Journal of Law, Economics, and Organization* Conference on Bureaucracy.

———. 1999. "Unilateral action and presidential power: A theory." *Presidential Studies Quarterly* 29:850–72.

Moe, Terry M., and Scott A. Wilson. 1994. "Presidents and the politics of structure." *Law and Contemporary Problems* 57:1–44.

Montinola, Gabriela. n.d. "Who guards the guardians? The institutional foundations of corruption." Manuscript, Stanford University.

Morgan, Ruth P. 1970. *The president and civil rights: Policy-making by executive order*. New York: St. Martin's Press.

Nathan, Richard P. 1975. *The plot that failed: Nixon and the administrative presidency*. New York: Wiley.

———. 1983. *The administrative presidency.* New York: Wiley.

National Biological Service (NBS). 1995. *The twenty most frequently asked questions about NBS.* January 10.

Nelson, Michael, ed. 1996. *Guide to the presidency.* Washington, D.C.: Congressional Quarterly Press.

Neustadt, Richard E. 1960. *Presidential power, the politics of leadership.* New York: Wiley.

Newman, Andrew Eric. 1991. "Institutional, political, and economic factors affecting rates of organizational change in California state government, 1850–1975." Ph.D. dissertation, Stanford University.

Noll, Roger G. 1971. *Reforming regulation: An evaluation of the Ash Council proposals.* Washington, D.C.: Brookings Institution Press.

Ornstein, Norman J., Thomas E. Mann, and Michael J. Malbin. 1998. *Vital statistics on Congress 1997–1998.* Washington, D.C.: American Enterprise Institute.

Ota, Alan K. 1999. "Appropriations concoct a VA-HUD bill, but full House, Senate may make changes." *CQ Weekly,* July 31, pp. 1864–66.

Peckenpaugh, Jason. 2002. "From the ground up." *Government Executive,* January 1.

Peters, Katherine McIntire. 2001. "The war at home." *Government Executive,* November 1.

Peterson, Gale E. 1985. *President Harry S. Truman and the independent regulatory commissions, 1945–1952.* New York: Garland.

Pincus, Walter. 1999a. "Official yields on nuclear oversight." *San Jose Mercury News,* July 8, p. A1.

———. 1999b. "Report warns of lab reform roadblocks." *Washington Post,* July 20, p. A5.

Pincus, Walter, and Vernon Loeb. 1999. "Support builds for separate nuclear authority." *Washington Post,* June 17, p. A18.

Pine, Art. 1999. "GOP firm on restructuring lab security." *San Jose Mercury News,* June 23, p. A16.

Poole, Keith. 1998. "Estimating a basic space from a set of issue scales." *American Journal of Political Science* 42:954–93.

President's Advisory Council on Executive Organization. 1972. *Establishment of a Department of Natural Resources–Organization for Social and Economic Progress.* Washington, D.C.: GPO.

President's Committee on Administrative Management. 1937. *Administrative management in the government of the United States.* Washington, D.C.: GPO.

President's Foreign Intelligence Advisory Board. 1999. *Science at its best, security at its worst: A report on security problems at the U.S. Department of Energy.*

Pulliam, H. Ronald. 1995. "The birth of a federal research agency." *Science and Biodiversity Policy,* Bioscience supplement: S-91-95.

———. 1998a. "The political education of a biologist, part I." *Wildlife Society Bulletin* 26:199-202.

———. 1998b. "The political education of a biologist, part II." *Wildlife Society Bulletin* 26:499-503.

Randall, Ronald. 1979. "Presidential powers versus bureaucratic intransigence: The influence of the Nixon administration on welfare policy." *American Political Science Review* 73:795-810.

Reich, Kenneth. 1995. "Babbitt assails GOP's plan to cut three agencies; Government: Interior secretary says U.S. Geological Survey's work crucial to understanding quakes." *Los Angeles Times,* February 2, part B, p. 11.

Risen, James. 1999. "Report scolds bureaucracy for U.S. Nuclear Lab lapses." *New York Times,* June 15.

Rivers, Douglas, and Nancy L. Rose. 1985. "Passing the president's program: Public opinion and presidential influence in Congress." *American Journal of Political Science* 29:183-96.

Rogers, W. H. 1993. "Regression standard errors in clustered samples." *Stata Technical Bulletin* 13:19-23.

Rohde, David W., and Dennis M. Simon. 1985. "Presidential vetoes and congressional response: A study of institutional conflict." *American Journal of Political Science* 29:397-427.

Rourke, Francis E. 1957. "The politics of administrative organization: A case history." *Journal of Politics* 19:461-78.

Segal, Jeffrey A., Charles M. Cameron, and Albert D. Cover. 1992. "A spatial model of roll call voting: Senators, constituents, presidents, and interest groups in Supreme Court confirmations." *American Journal of Political Science* 36(1):96-121.

Seidman, Harold. 1981. "A typology of government." In *Federal reorganization: What have we learned?* edited by Peter Szanton. Chatham, N.J.: Chatham House.

———. 1998. *Politics, position, and power: The dynamics of federal organization.* New York: Oxford University Press.

Skowronek, Stephen. 1993. *The politics presidents make: Leadership from John Adams to George Bush.* Cambridge: Harvard University Press, Belknap Press.

Stanley, David T. 1965. *Changing administrations: The 1961 and 1964 transitions in six departments.* Washington, D.C.: Brookings Institution Press.

StataCorp. 1997. *Stata Statistical Software: Release 5.0*. College Station, Tex.: Stata Corporation.

Stewart, Joseph, Jr., and Jane S. Cromartie. 1982. "Partisan presidential change and regulatory policy: The case of the FTC and deceptive practices enforcement, 1938–1974." *Presidential Studies Quarterly* 12:568–73.

Stinchcombe, Arthur L. 1965. "Social structures and organizations." In *Handbook of Organizations*, edited by J. G. March, pp. 142–93. Chicago: Rand McNally.

Szanton, Peter, ed. 1981. *Federal reorganization: What have we learned?* Chatham, N.J.: Chatham House.

Towell, Pat. 1999a. "Nuclear agency eruption." *CQ Weekly*, October 9, p. 2399.

———. 1999b. "Administration has few options on nuclear agency, study says." *CQ Weekly*, November 6, p. 2670.

Truman, Harry S. 1946. *Public papers of the presidents of the United States: Harry S. Truman, 1945–1953*. 8 vols. Washington, D.C.: GPO.

Tuma, Nancy Brandon, and Michael T. Hannan. 1984. *Social dynamics: Models and methods*. Orlando, Fla.: Academic Press.

U.S. Commission on National Security/21st Century. 2001. "Road map for national security: Imperative for change." Final draft report, January 31.

U.S. Department of Interior. 1993. *Order no. 3173*. September 29.

U.S. Department of Interior. 1994. *Fact sheet: The facts on the National Biological Survey*. June 8.

U.S. Department of Interior. 1996. *Order no. 3202*. September 30.

U.S. House. 1970. *Hearings before the Subcommittee of the House Committee on Government Operations*, part 1. 91st Cong., 2nd sess.

U.S. House. 1993a. *Hearing before the Subcommittee on Technology, Environment, and Aviation and the Subcommittee on Investigations and Oversight of the Committee on Science, Space, and Technology on H.R. 1845— The National Biological Survey Act of 1993*. 103rd Cong., 1st sess.

U.S. House. 1993b. *Report 103–193. National Biological Survey Act of 1993*. 103rd Cong., 1st sess.

U.S. House. 1995. *Hearing before the Subcommittee on Environment and Natural Resources joint with Subcommittee on Fisheries Management of the Committee on Merchant Marine and Fisheries on the NMFS, FWS, and NBS Budgets for FY 1995*. 103rd Cong., 1st sess.

U.S. House. 1999. Committee on Commerce, Subcommittee on Oversight and Investigations. *Security at the Department of Energy's laboratories: The perspective of the General Accounting Office*. 106th Cong., 1st sess., April 20.

U.S. House. 2000a. Armed Services Committee. Special panel on Department of Energy reorganization. *Department of Energy National Nuclear Security Administration Implementation Plan: An assessment.* 106th Cong., 2nd sess., February.

U.S. House. 2000b. Committee on Armed Services Special Oversight Panel on Department of Energy Reorganization. *Establishing the National Nuclear Security Administration: A Year of Obstacles and Opportunities.* 106th Cong., 2nd sess., October 13.

Waterman, Richard W. 1989. *Presidential influence and the administrative state.* Knoxville: University of Tennessee Press.

Weko, Thomas J. 1995. *The politicizing presidency: The White House Personnel Office.* Lawrence: University Press of Kansas.

White, H. 1980. "A heteroskedasticity-consistent covariance matrix estimator and a direct test for heteroskedasticity." *Econometrica* 48:817–30.

———. 1982. "Maximum likelihood estimation of misspecified models." *Econometrica* 50:1–25.

Whitnah, Donald R. 1983. *Government agencies.* Westport, Conn.: Greenwood.

Wolanin, Thomas R. 1975. *Presidential advisory commissions: Truman to Nixon.* Madison: University of Wisconsin Press.

Wood, B. Dan. 1990. "Does politics make a difference at the EEOC?" *American Journal of Political Science* 34:503–30.

Wood, B. Dan, and James E. Anderson. 1993. "The politics of U.S. antitrust regulation." *American Journal of Political Science* 37:1–39.

Wood, B. Dan, and Richard W. Waterman. 1991. "The dynamics of political control of the bureaucracy." *American Political Science Review* 85:801–28.

———. 1994. *Bureaucratic dynamics: The role of bureaucracy in a democracy.* Boulder, Colo.: Westview Press.

Zegart, Amy Beth. 1999. *Flawed by design: The evolution of the CIA, JCS, and NSC.* Stanford, Calif.: Stanford University Press.

Index

administrative agency design, *see* agency design

administrative discretion, presidential use of, *see* executive action, agencies created by

Administrative Management, President's Committee on (1937), 7, 11, 27

administrative procedures, 9–10, 13, 17

Administrative Procedures Act (APA), 10, 40, 42

advisory bodies, 173

Advisory Council on Executive Organization (1972), 27

agency design, *see also* more specific topics: different types and preferences, value of, 160–61; duplication and overlap, 7–8, 28, 196n2; function of agency and, 12; future of, 166–67; theory of, 16–18, 166–67; variations, sources of, 15

Agricultural Credit Agency, 33

Agricultural Economics, Bureau of (BAE), 142

Agricultural Marketing Service, 142

Agricultural Research Service, 142

Agricultural Stabilization and Conservation Service, 139

Agriculture Department, *see* Department of Agriculture

Alcohol, Tobacco, and Firearms, Bureau of (ATF), 80, 98

Allard, Wayne, 95

American Bankers Association, 34

Amtrak, 44, 45, 142

Antiquities Act, 192n7

appointed positions, *see* fixed-term appointments; political appointments and appointees

appropriations, 76, 81–86; Department of the Interior, 95–96; existing accounts, using, 82–83; National Biological Service, 88, 93; new accounts, creating, 84–86; termination of agencies, 139

approval ratings, presidential, 56–58; Congressional success and, 86; executive-created agencies, 102–4; presidential strength and legislative influence, 124–25, 128–34

Architect of the Capitol, 44

archives, 41, 171–72

Arms Control and Disarmament Administration, 139

Ash Council, 11, 140

Asian Development Bank, 173

Atomic Energy Commission, 47, 108, 195n4

authorization of new agencies by Congress, 82, 192n8

Aviation and Transportation Security Act, 159

Babbitt, Bruce, 92–94, 96–97, 105

banking regulation, agencies controlling, 8

Benson, Ezra Taft, 141, 142

Bill of Rights, 2

Bingaman, Jeff, 111, 114, 117, 119

Biological Resources Division (BRD), 96–97

Biological Service, *see* National Biological Service

Biological Survey, Bureau of, 92

bivariate probit models, 58

boards or commissions, governance by, 46–48; durability of agencies, 145, 155, 197n10; presidents not likely to create agencies with, 90; variable for models of agency insulation, 59

Boland Amendment, 25

Border Patrol, 77

Botanic Garden, 44

Brownlow Commission, 11, 140, 163

Bryan, Richard, 119

Budget and Accounting Acts of 1921 and 1974, 25

Budget Enforcement Act of 1990, 25, 177

budgetary control of agencies, 9–10, 17, 46; appropriations, *see* appropriations; average budgets for legislatively created vs. executive-created agencies, 89; National Biological Service and BRD, 95–97; OMB, *see* Office of Management and Budget (OMB); self-financed agencies, 144; size and complexity of budget, repercussions of, 85

Bureau of Agricultural Economics (BAE), 142

Bureau of Alcohol, Tobacco, and Firearms (ATF), 80, 98

Bureau of Biological Survey, 92

Bureau of Immigration Enforcement, 138

Bureau of Indian Affairs, 8

Bureau of Mines, 72

Bureau of the Budget, 71, *see also* Office of Management and Budget (OMB)

bureaucracy design, *see* agency design

Burford, Anne, 138

Bush, George H. W., and administration, 54, 71, 86

Bush, George W., and administration, 76, 77–78

cabinet departments, *see also* individual departments: agencies outside or within, *see* independent regulatory commissions vs. cabinet department control; secretarial/departmental action, agencies created by, 79–80, 124–27

Carnegie Commission, 92

Carpenter, Daniel, 145, 197n7

Carter, Jimmy, and administration, 49, 54–55, 73

Case Act, 25

Central Intelligence Agency (CIA), 8, 109, 110

Central Security Service, 79, 98, 195n14

China, 109, 110

civil rights administration by executive action, 76–77

Civil Service Commission, 85

Clean Air Act, 10

Clinton, Bill, and administration: accountability and authority of cabinet department heads, 107, 115; Antiquities Act, use of, 192n7; consolidation of banking regulation functions, 140; National Biological Service, *see* National Biological Service; NNSA, *see* National Nuclear Security Agency (NNSA); number of agencies created under, 54; Office of Religious Persecution Monitoring, 73

coalitions, *see* partisan politics and coalitions

Coast Guard, 77

Commerce Department, 34, 48, 73, 142

Printed and bound by CPI Group (UK) Ltd, Croydon, CR0 4YY

23/04/2025

14660940-0001